More journals from this author:
Know Your Feelings Journal
Daily Reflection Challenge Journal
Feeling Myself Journal
Before & After Therapy Tracking Journal

olivetreehealthllc.com

Paperback ISBN: 979-8-9882406-0-0

Feelings are not Facts
Journal Overview

It can be really hard to separate your feelings from what you really need to focus on.

This journal will help you do just that.

It can be helpful to remember you are not your emotions- **you are just experiencing an emotion.**

Once you ride the wave of the emotion, you often come out with more clarity, presence, and confidence.

Happy emoting!

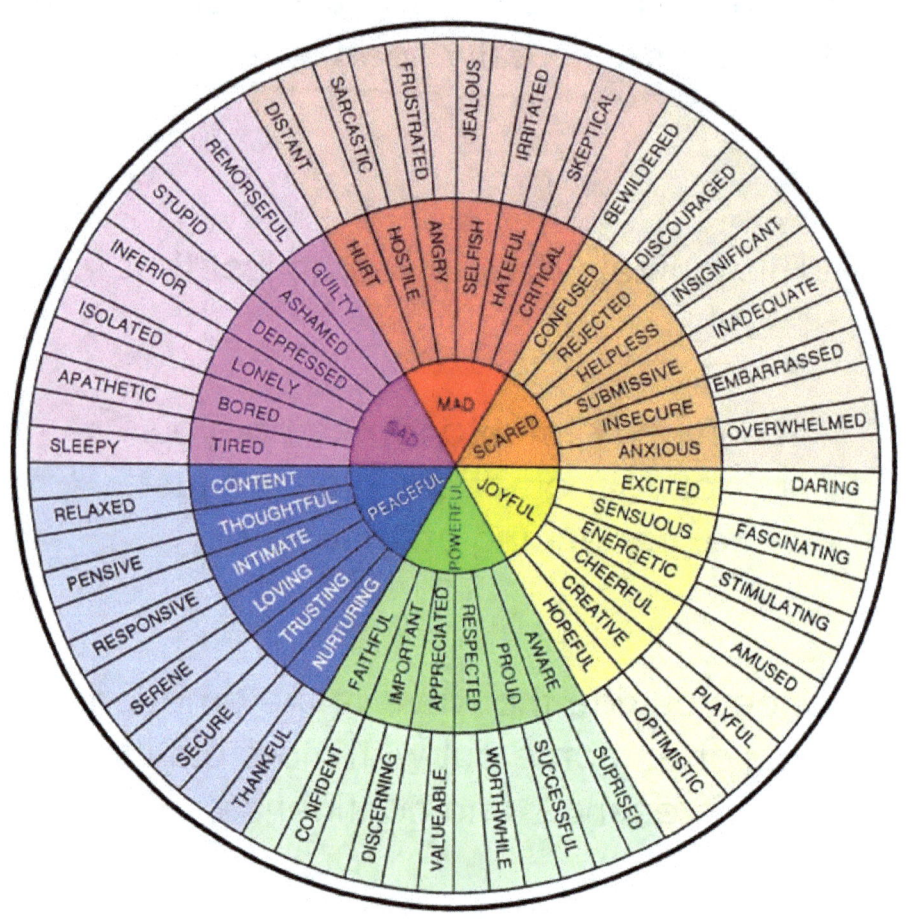

Feelings Chart

Situation that triggered the emotions:

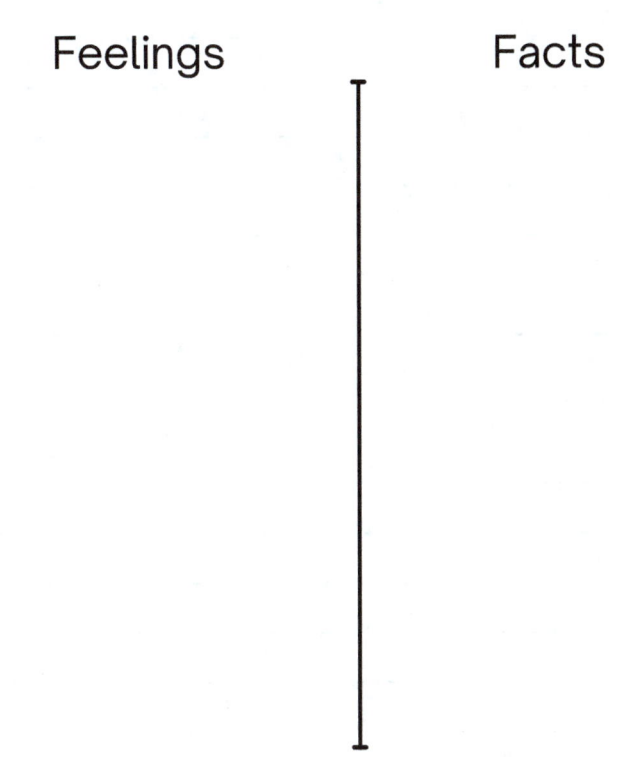

Feelings   Facts

Comforting thought to hold on to:

ituation that triggered the emotions:

Feelings   Facts

Comforting thought to hold on to:

Situation that triggered the emotions:

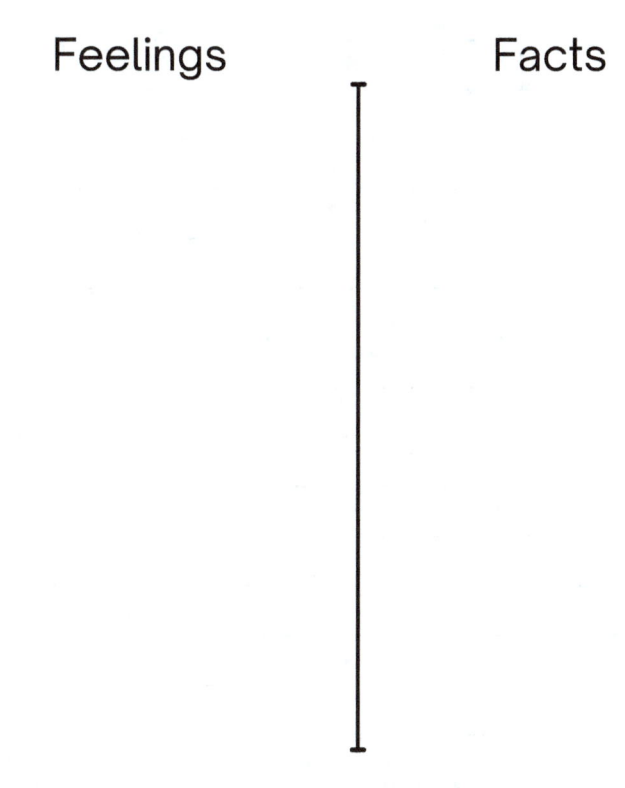

Feelings   Facts

Comforting thought to hold on to:

Situation that triggered the emotions:

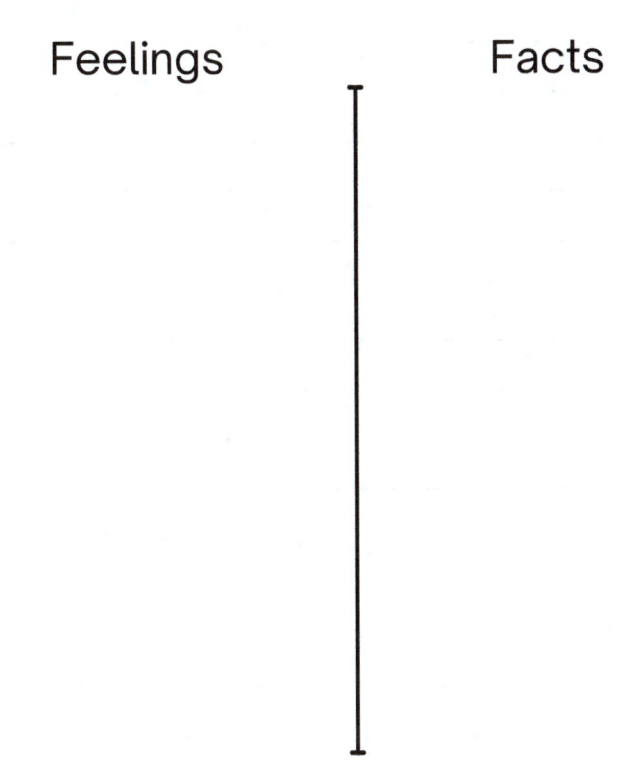

Feelings   Facts

Comforting thought to hold on to:

ituation that triggered the emotions:

Feelings   Facts

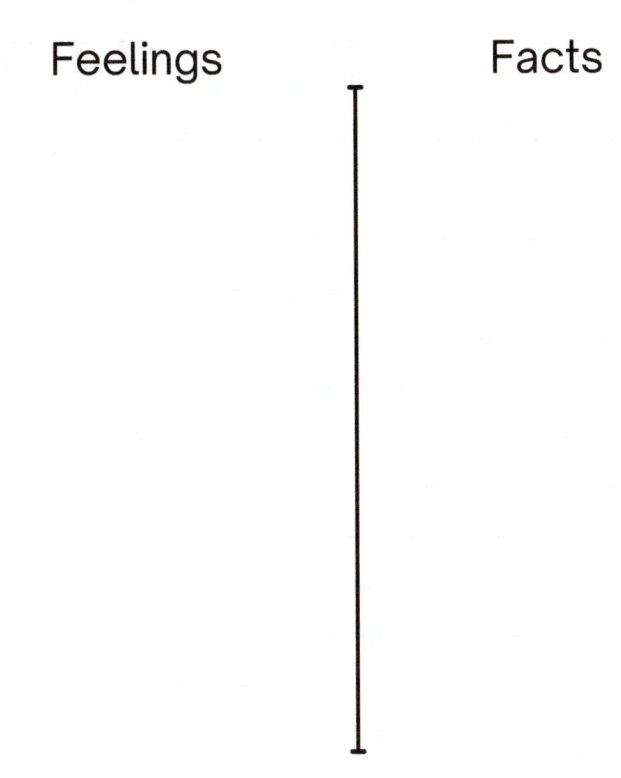

Comforting thought to hold on to:

Situation that triggered the emotions:

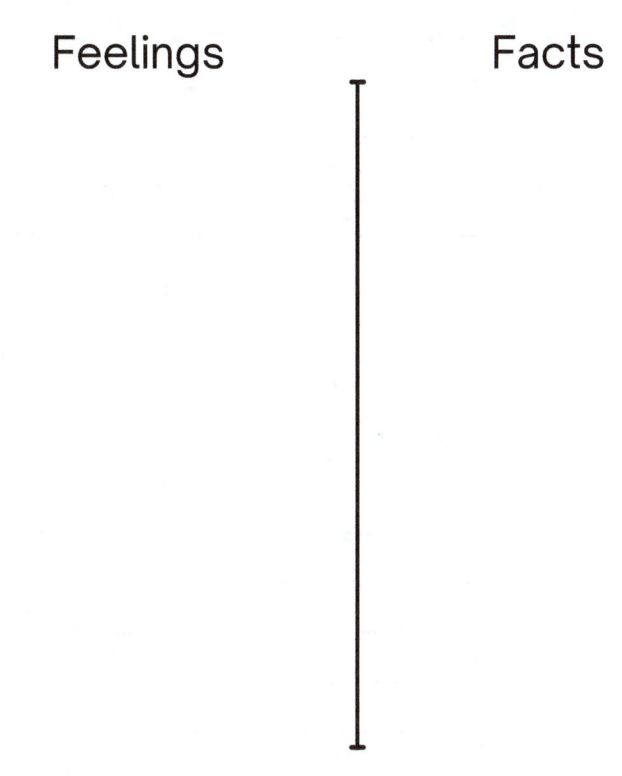

Feelings   Facts

Comforting thought to hold on to:

Situation that triggered the emotions:

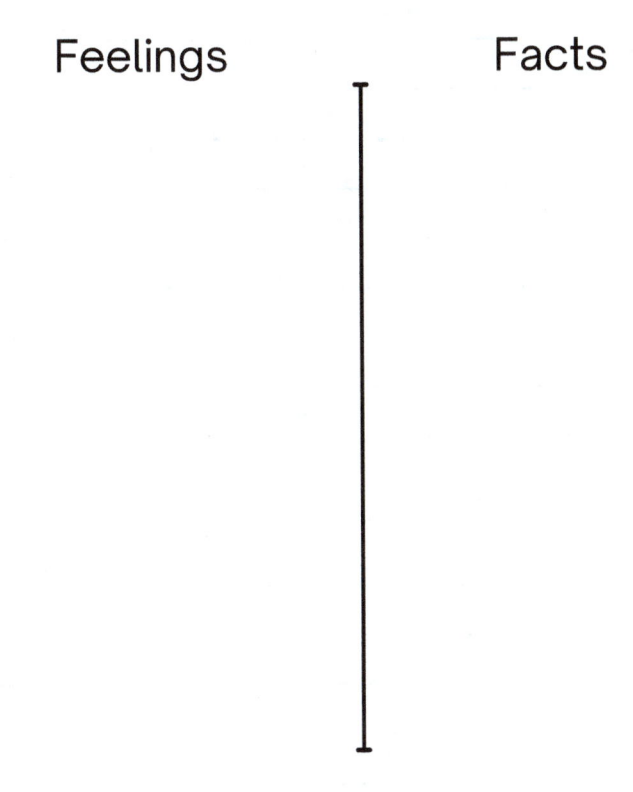

Feelings   Facts

Comforting thought to hold on to:

tuation that triggered the emotions:

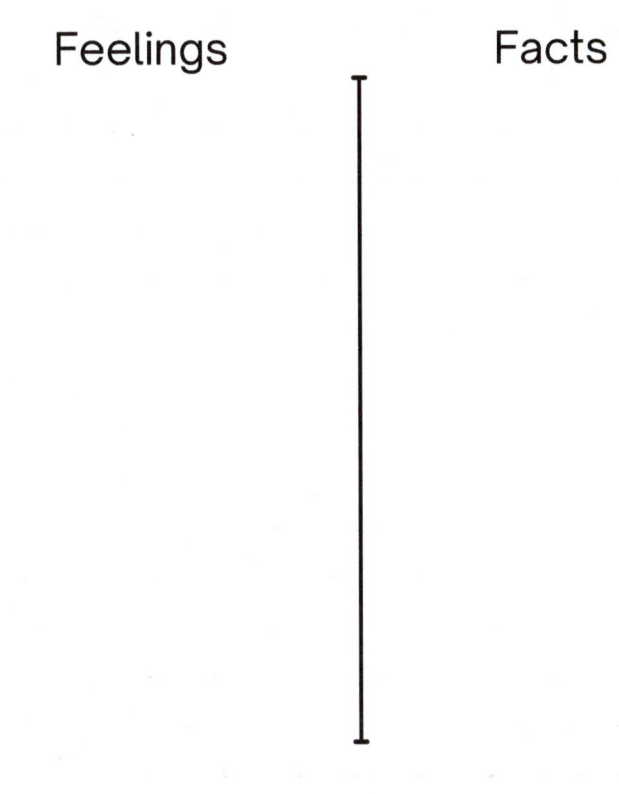

Feelings   Facts

Comforting thought to hold on to:

Situation that triggered the emotions:

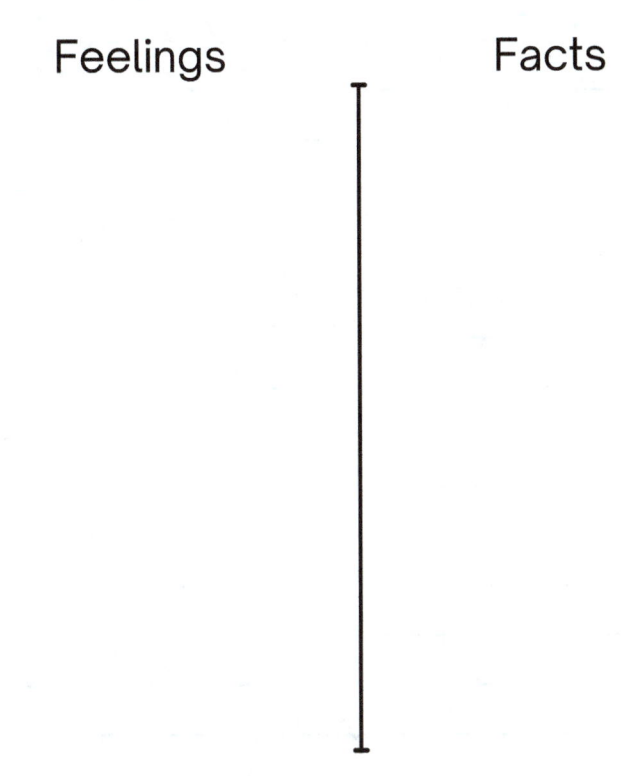

Feelings   Facts

Comforting thought to hold on to:

Situation that triggered the emotions:

Feelings   Facts

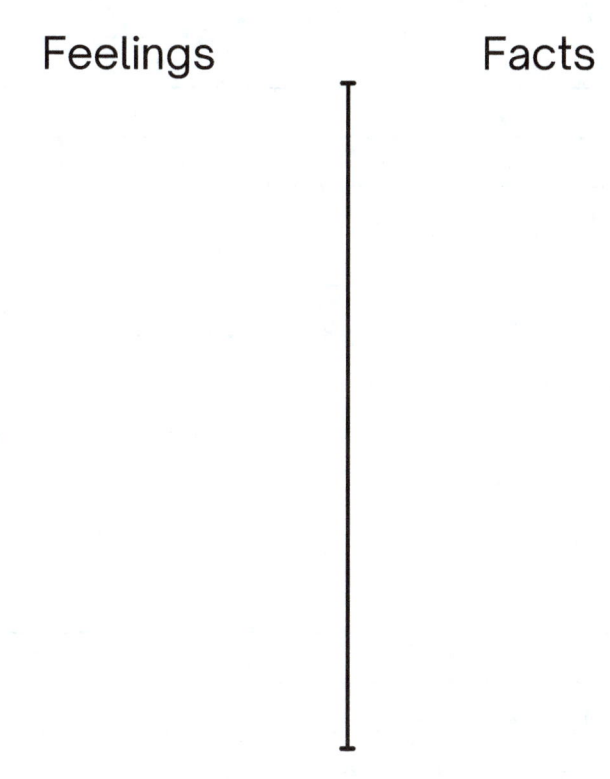

Comforting thought to hold on to:

tuation that triggered the emotions:

Feelings   Facts

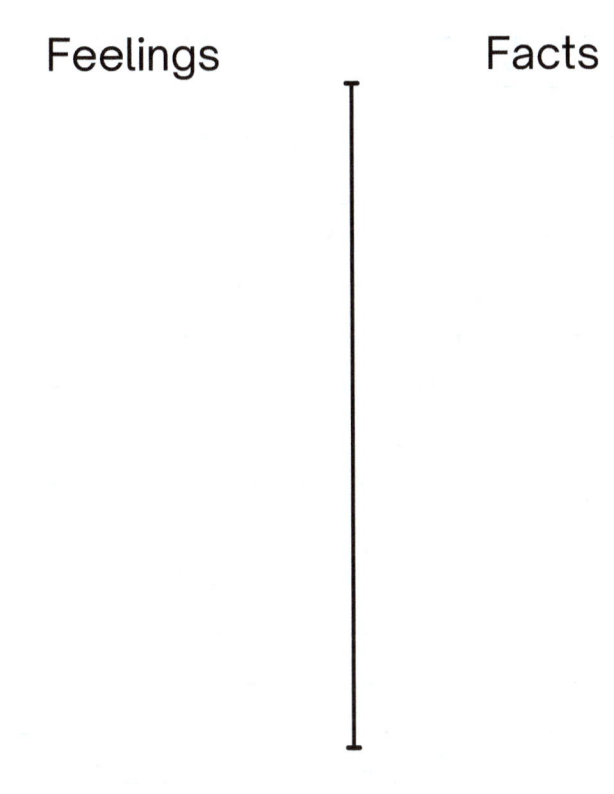

Comforting thought to hold on to:

Situation that triggered the emotions:

Feelings   Facts

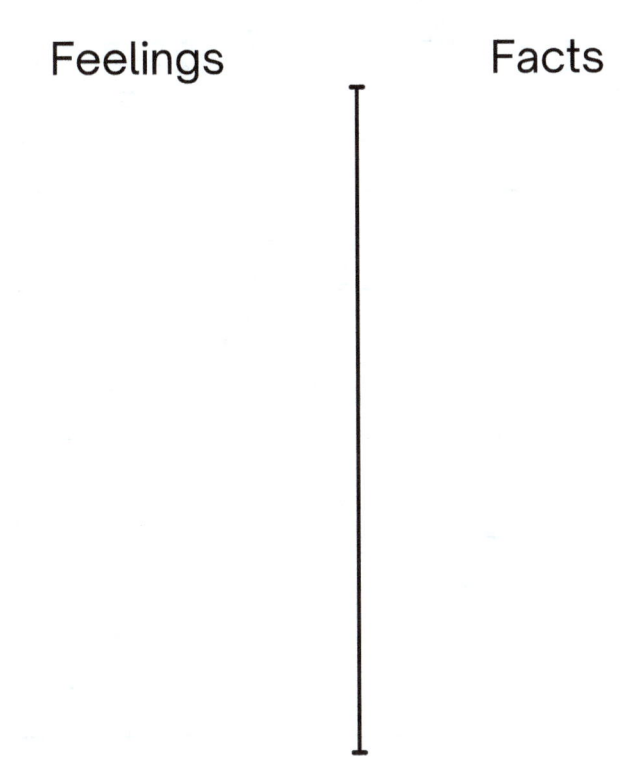

Comforting thought to hold on to:

Situation that triggered the emotions:

Feelings   Facts

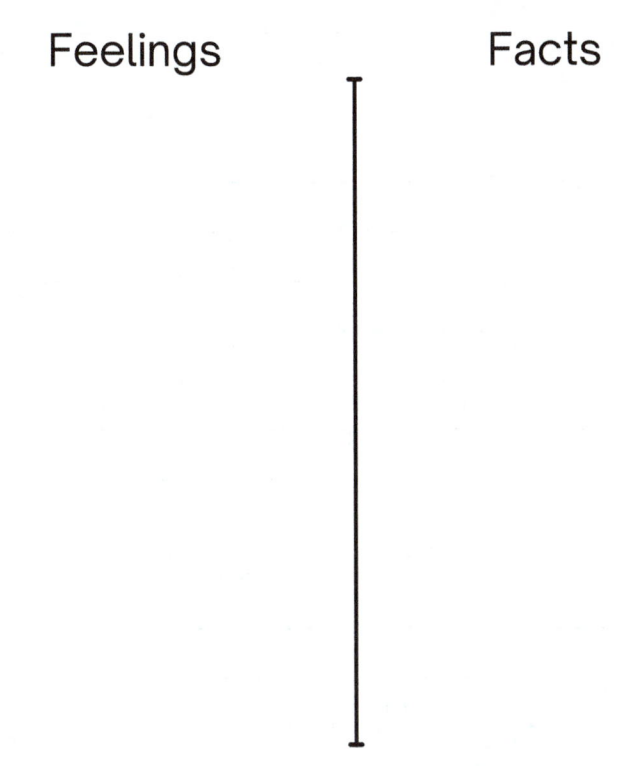

Comforting thought to hold on to:

tuation that triggered the emotions:

Feelings   Facts

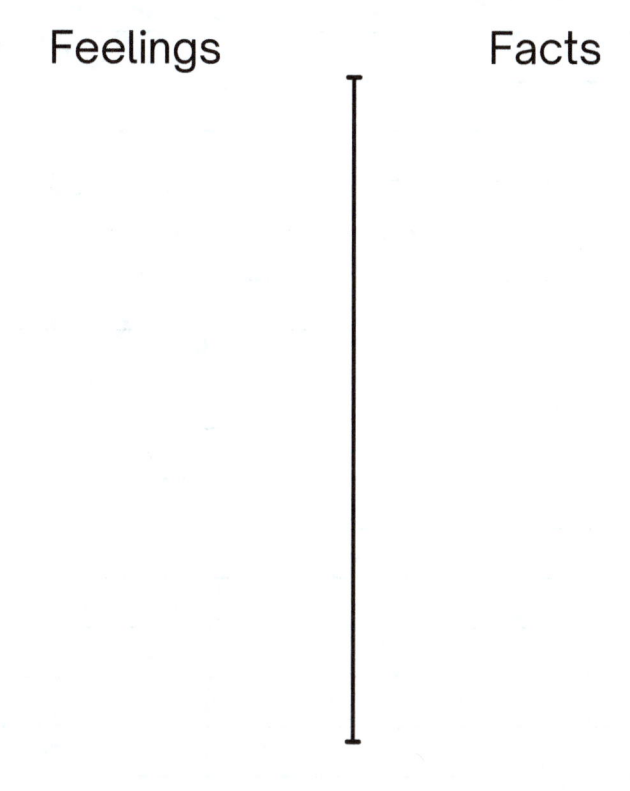

Comforting thought to hold on to:

Situation that triggered the emotions:

Feelings

Facts

Comforting thought to hold on to:

Situation that triggered the emotions:

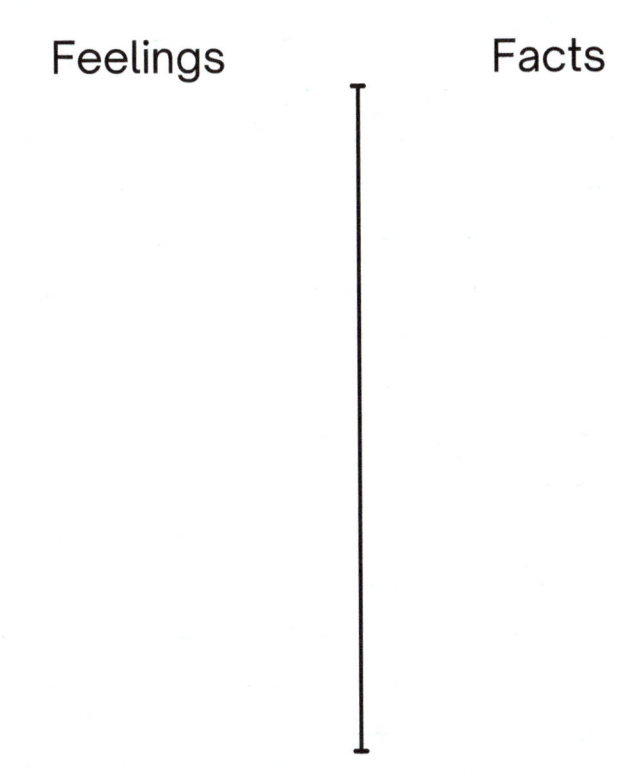

Feelings   Facts

Comforting thought to hold on to:

tuation that triggered the emotions:

Feelings   Facts

Comforting thought to hold on to:

Situation that triggered the emotions:

Feelings   Facts

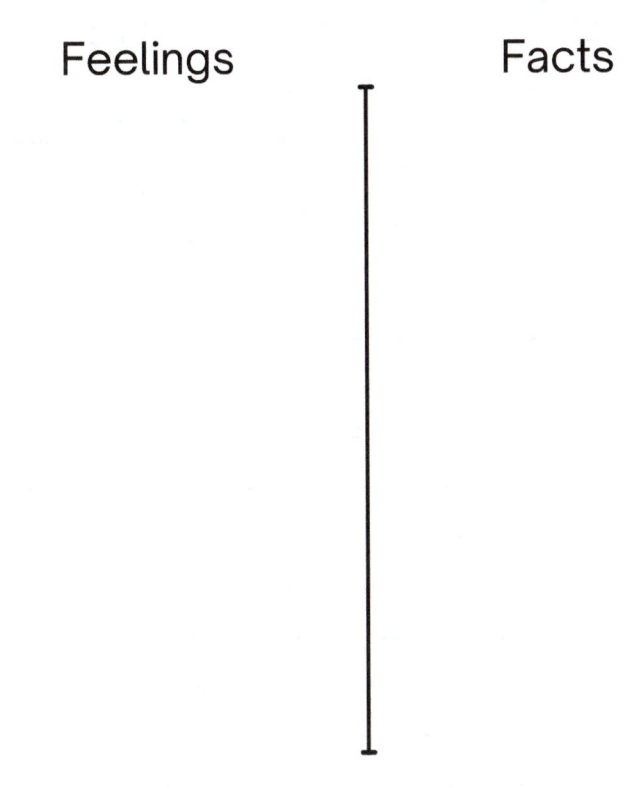

Comforting thought to hold on to:

Situation that triggered the emotions:

Feelings   Facts

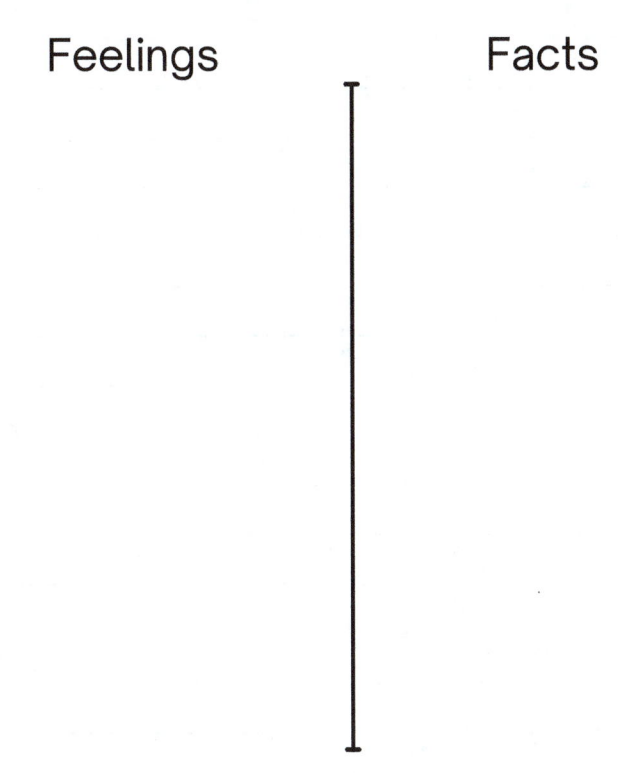

Comforting thought to hold on to:

tuation that triggered the emotions:

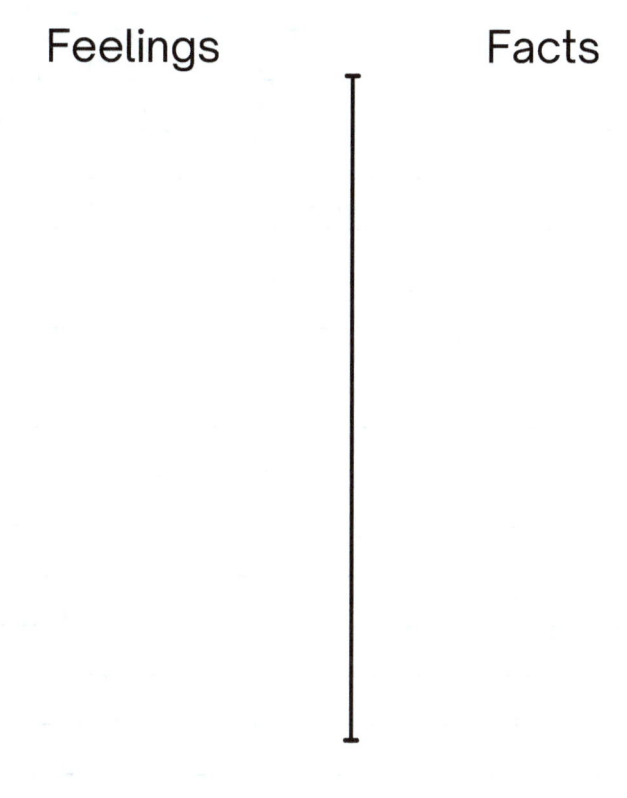

Feelings   Facts

Comforting thought to hold on to:

Situation that triggered the emotions:

Feelings   Facts

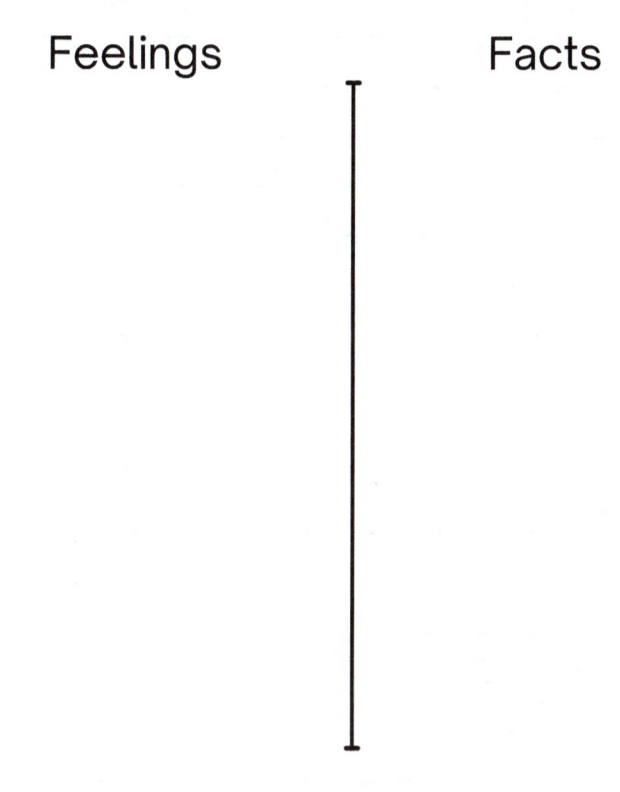

Comforting thought to hold on to:

Situation that triggered the emotions:

Feelings   Facts

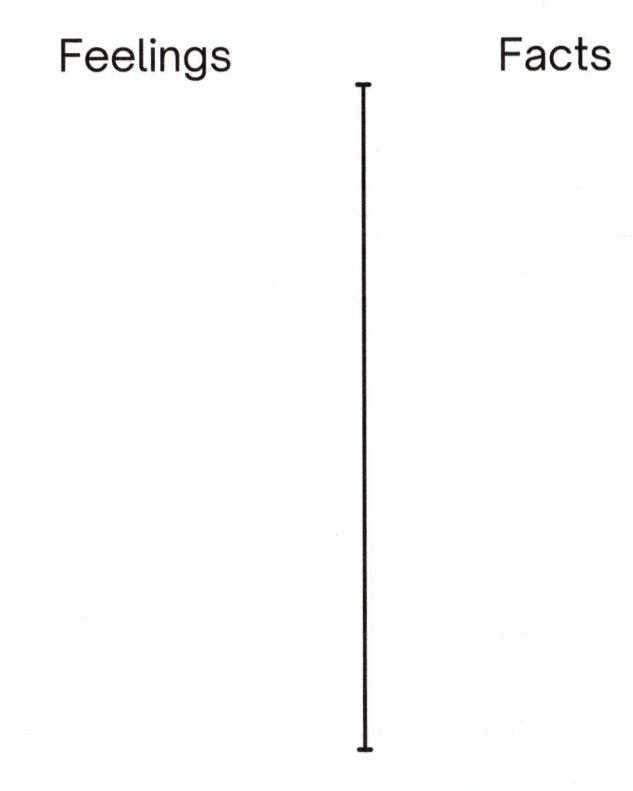

Comforting thought to hold on to:

tuation that triggered the emotions:

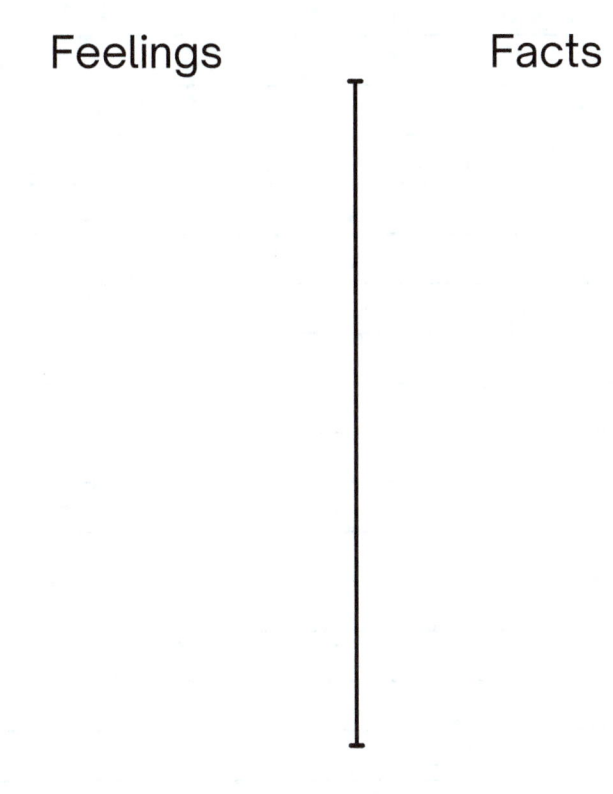

Feelings   Facts

Comforting thought to hold on to:

Situation that triggered the emotions:

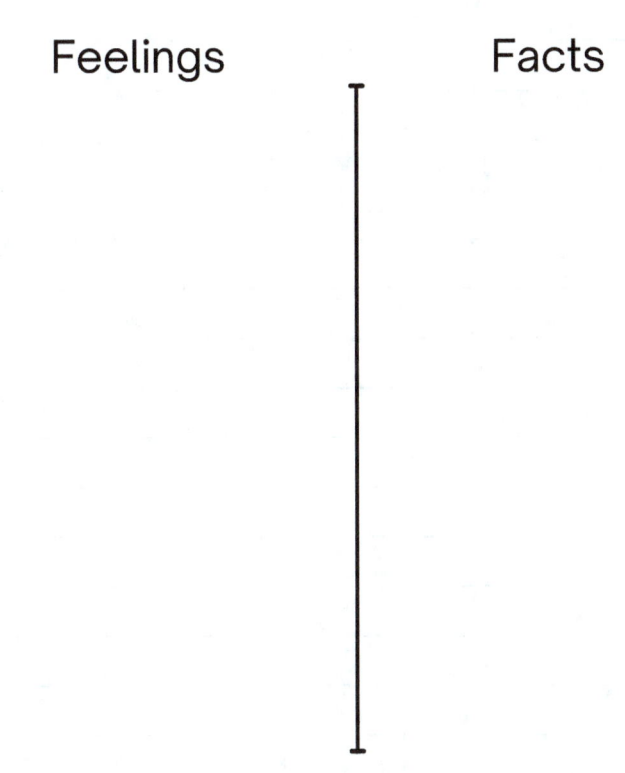

Feelings   Facts

Comforting thought to hold on to:

Situation that triggered the emotions:

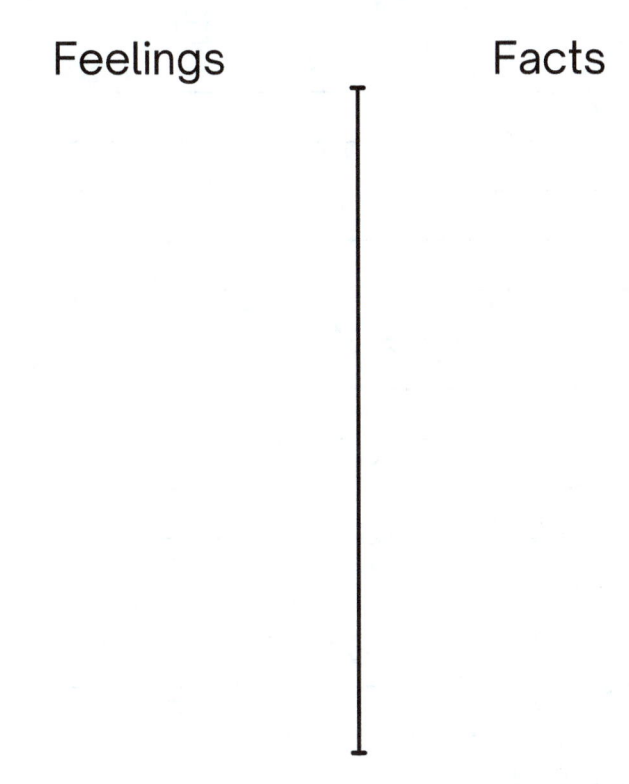

Feelings   Facts

Comforting thought to hold on to:

tuation that triggered the emotions:

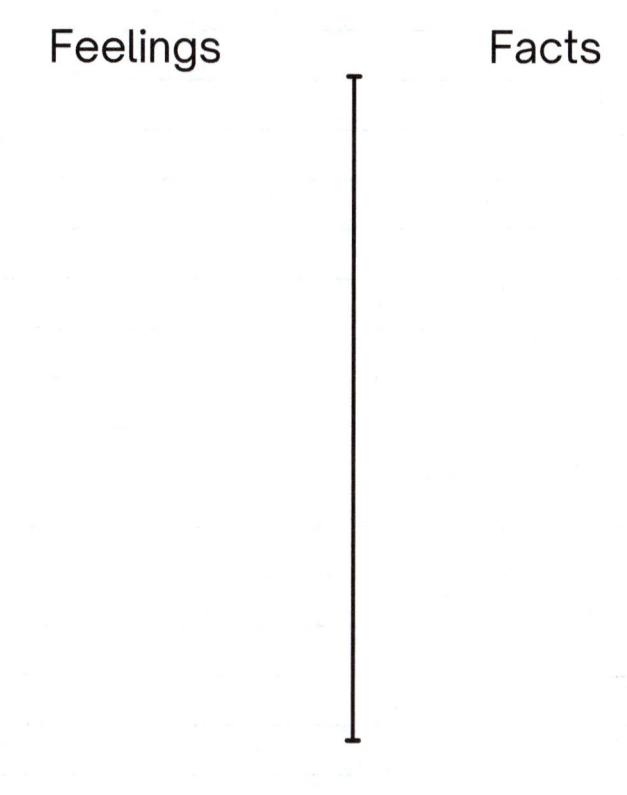

Feelings   Facts

Comforting thought to hold on to:

Situation that triggered the emotions:

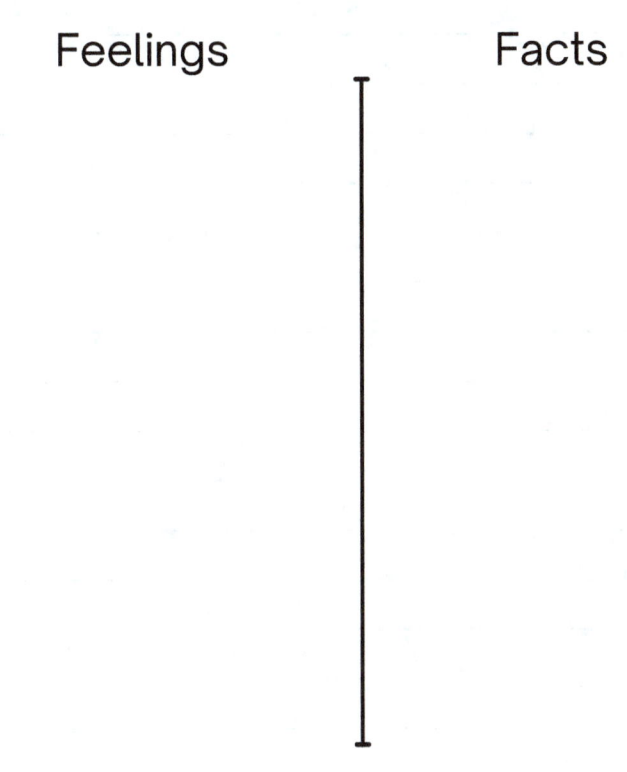

Feelings   Facts

Comforting thought to hold on to:

ituation that triggered the emotions:

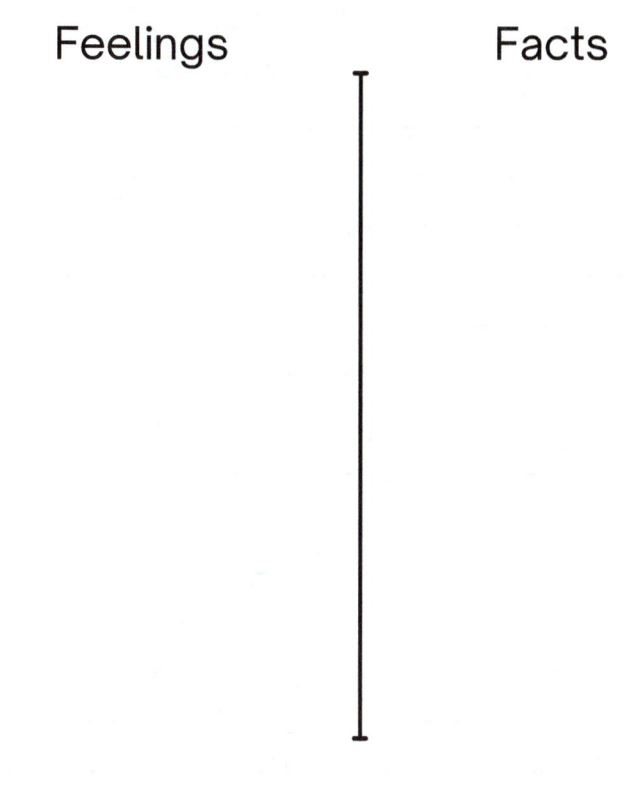

Feelings   Facts

Comforting thought to hold on to:

tuation that triggered the emotions:

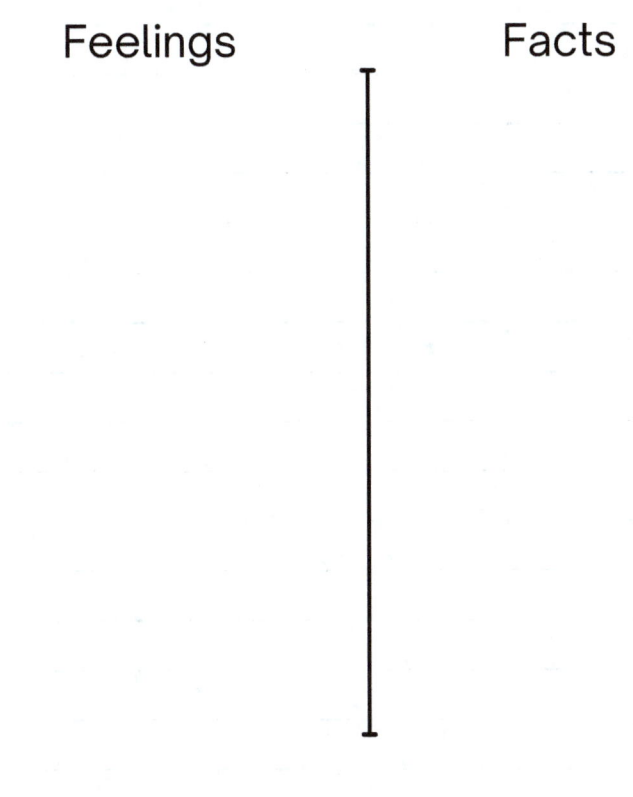

Feelings   Facts

Comforting thought to hold on to:

Situation that triggered the emotions:

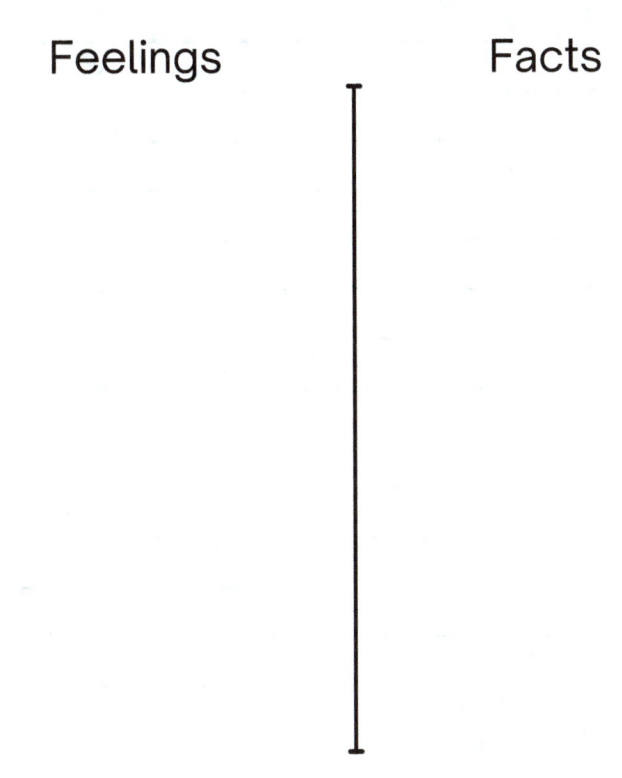

Feelings   Facts

Comforting thought to hold on to:

Situation that triggered the emotions:

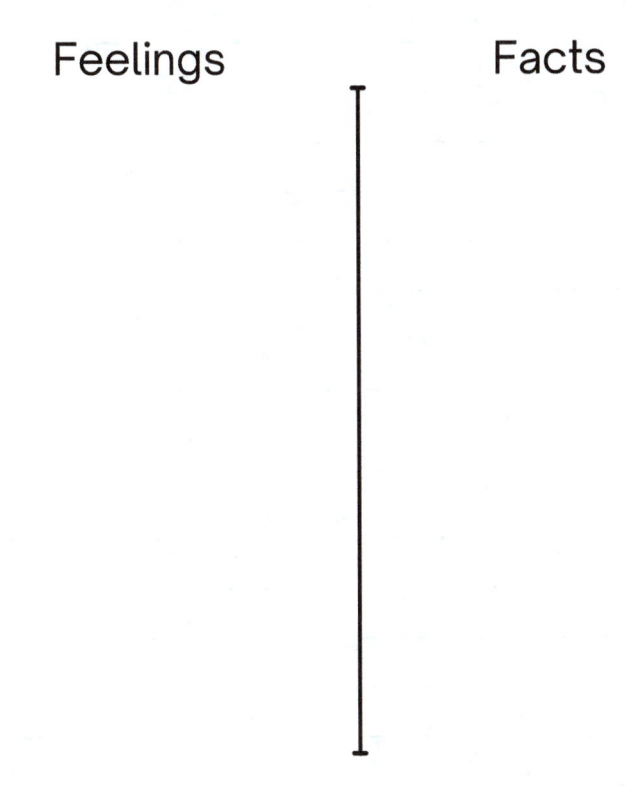

Feelings   Facts

Comforting thought to hold on to:

tuation that triggered the emotions:

Feelings   Facts

Comforting thought to hold on to:

Situation that triggered the emotions:

Feelings   Facts

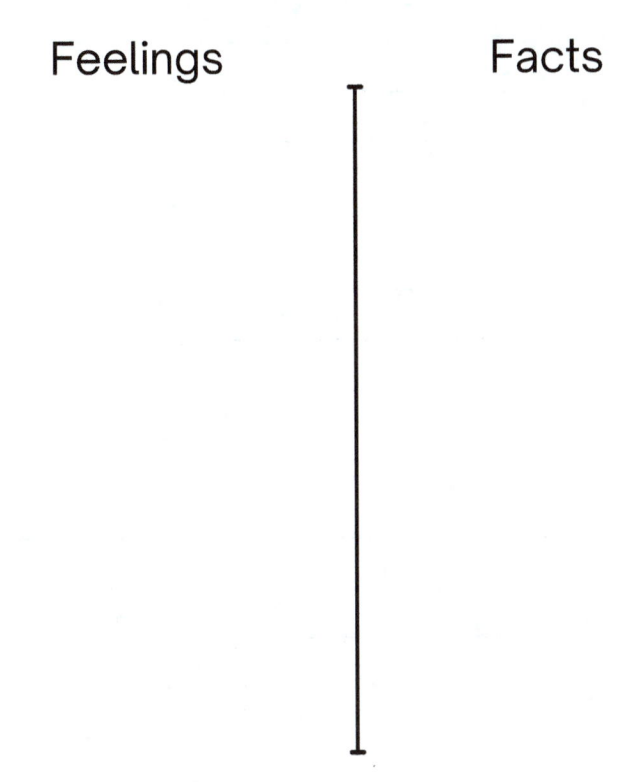

Comforting thought to hold on to:

ituation that triggered the emotions:

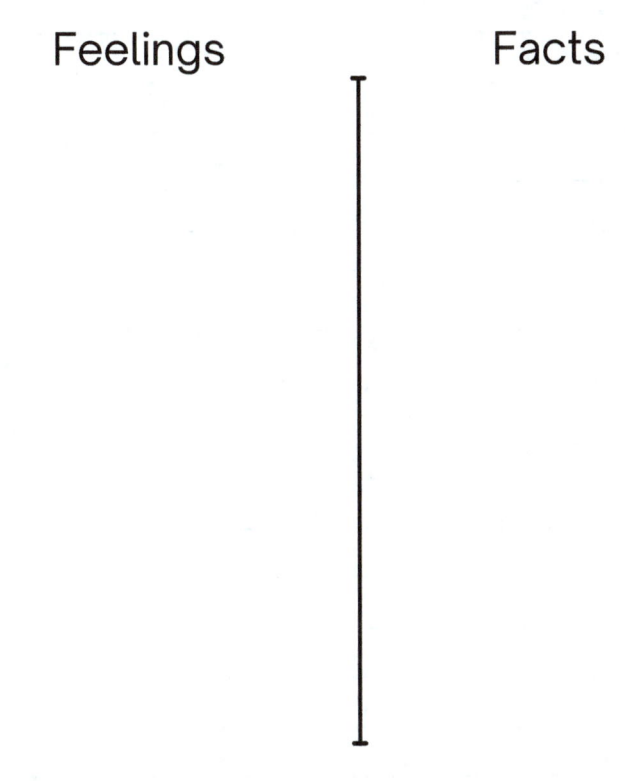

Feelings   Facts

Comforting thought to hold on to:

tuation that triggered the emotions:

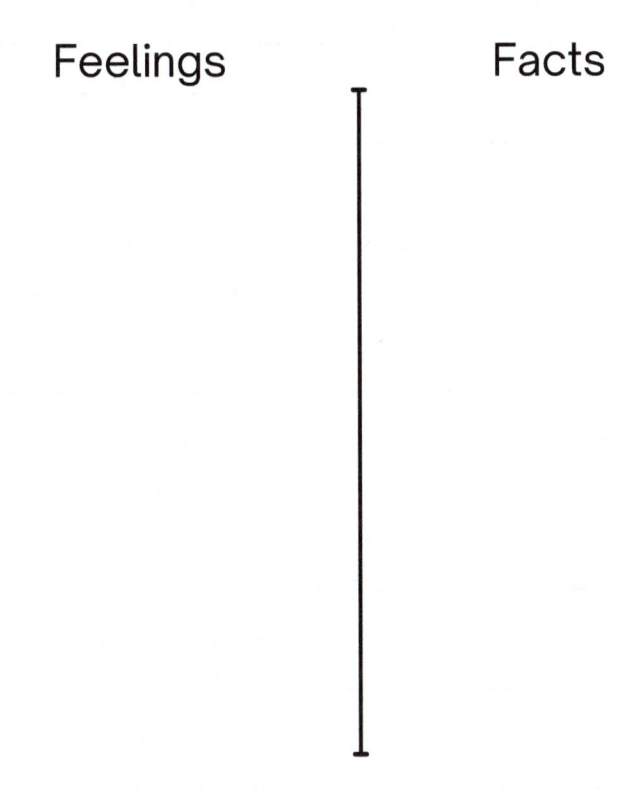

Feelings   Facts

Comforting thought to hold on to:

Situation that triggered the emotions:

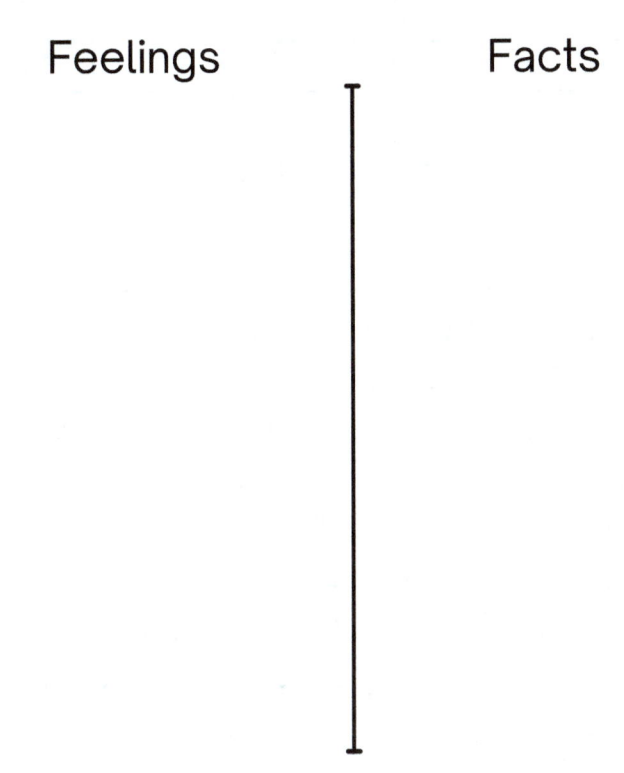

Feelings   Facts

Comforting thought to hold on to:

Situation that triggered the emotions:

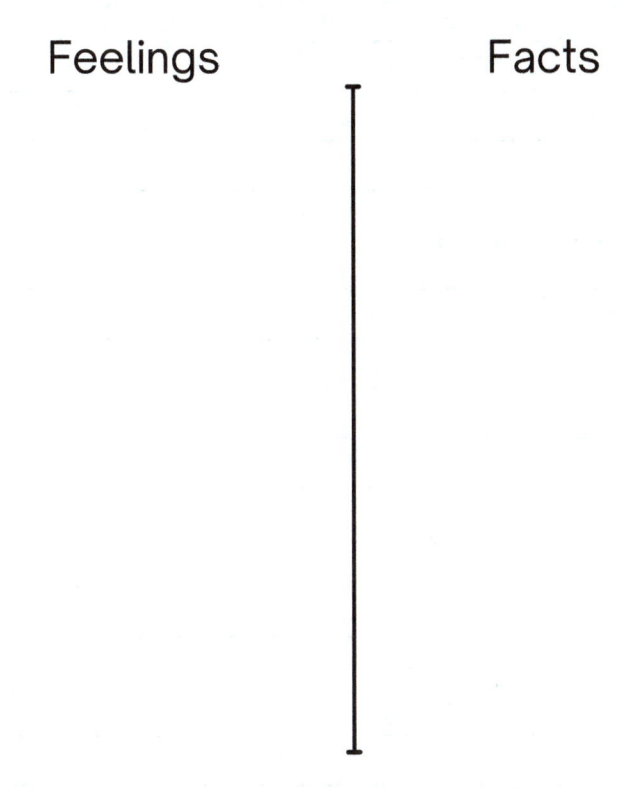

Feelings   Facts

Comforting thought to hold on to:

tuation that triggered the emotions:

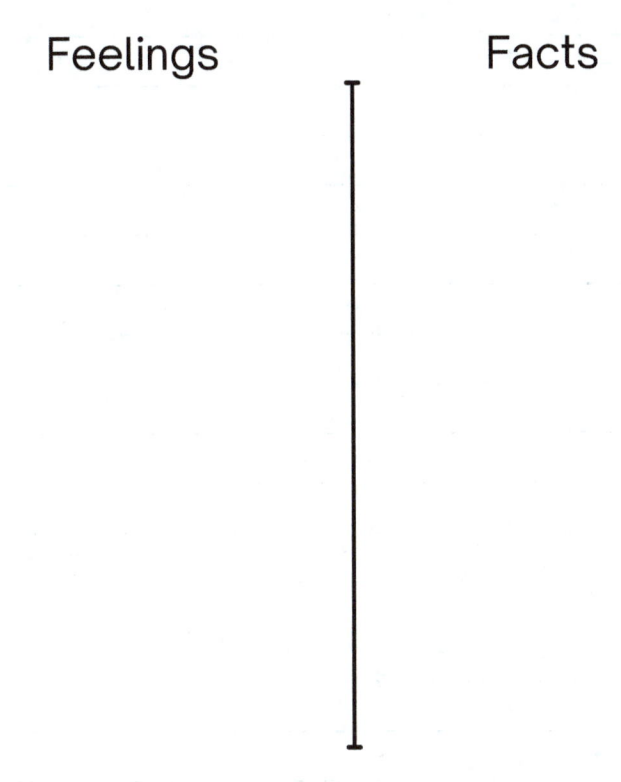

Feelings   Facts

Comforting thought to hold on to:

Situation that triggered the emotions:

Feelings   Facts

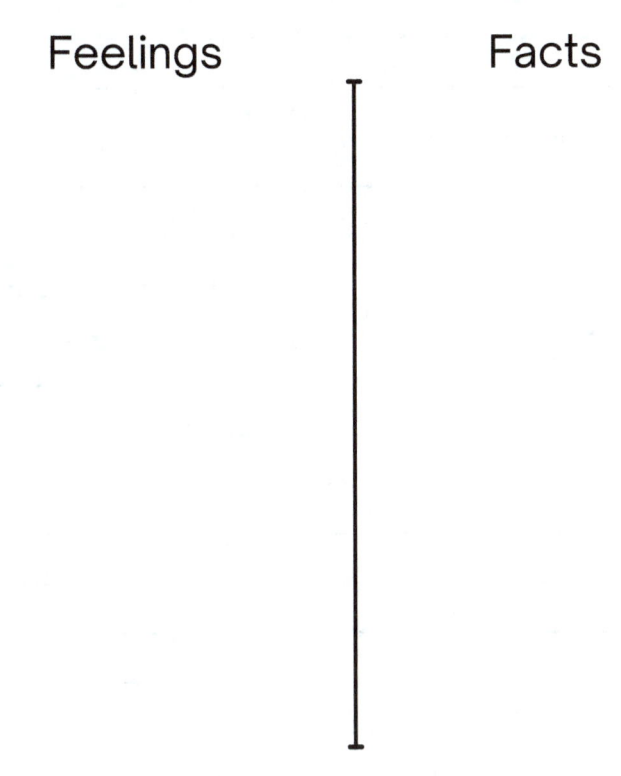

Comforting thought to hold on to:

ituation that triggered the emotions:

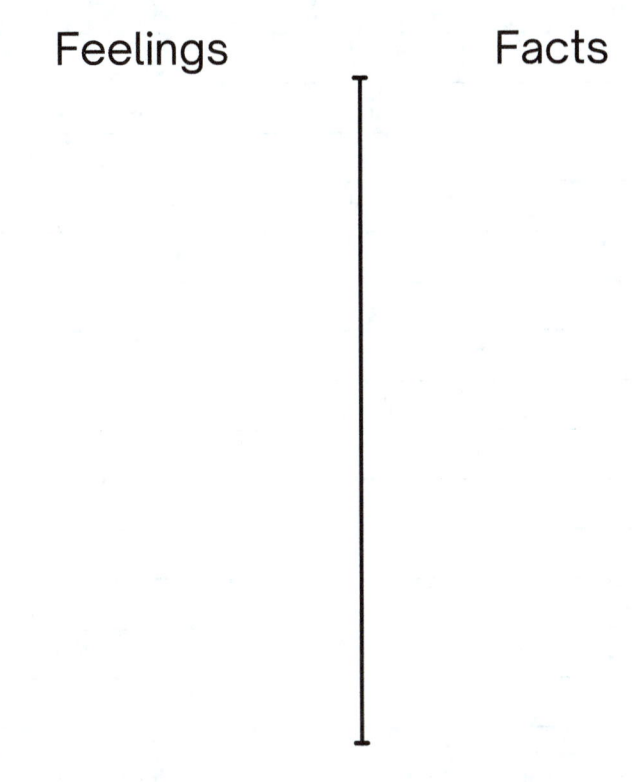

Feelings   Facts

Comforting thought to hold on to:

tuation that triggered the emotions:

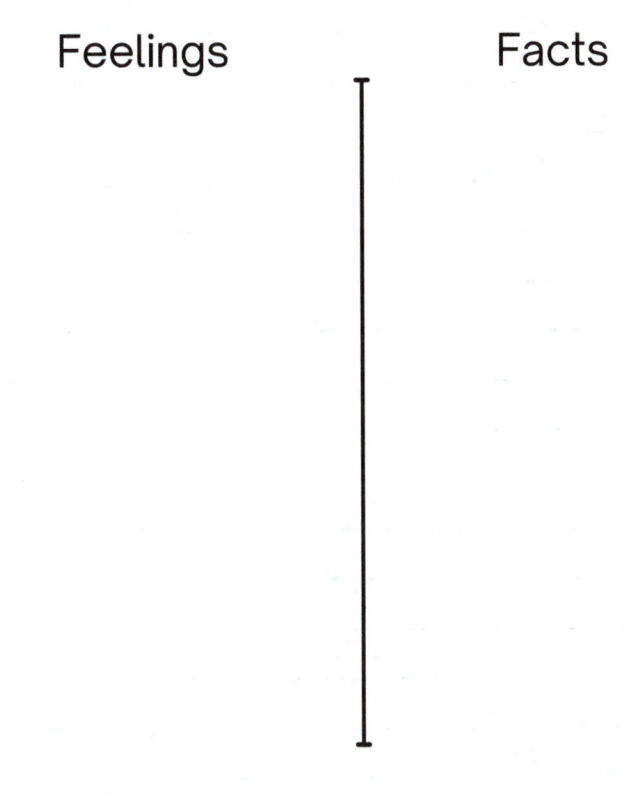

Feelings   Facts

Comforting thought to hold on to:

Situation that triggered the emotions:

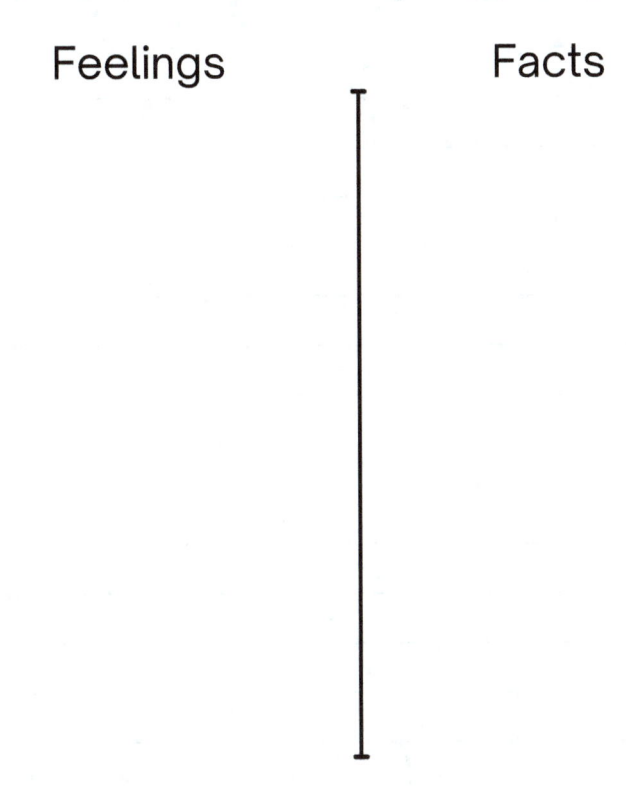

Feelings   Facts

Comforting thought to hold on to:

Situation that triggered the emotions:

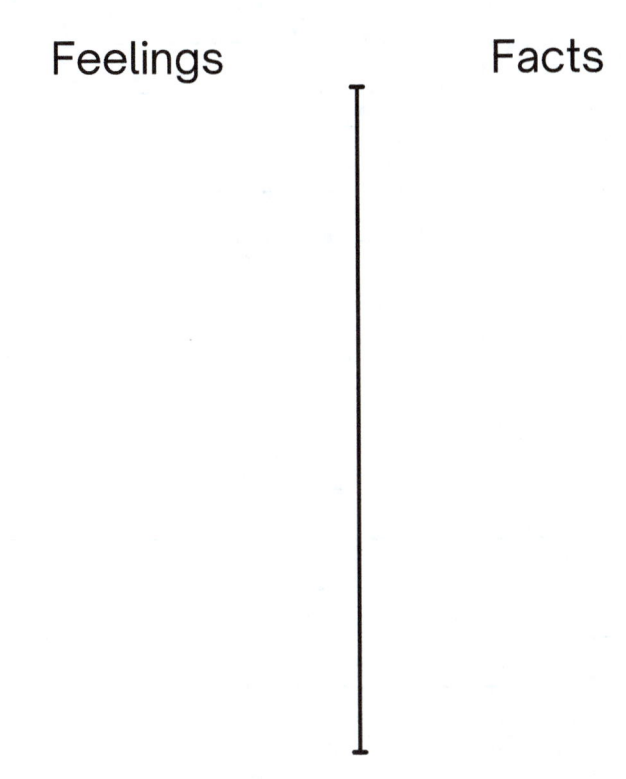

Feelings   Facts

Comforting thought to hold on to:

tuation that triggered the emotions:

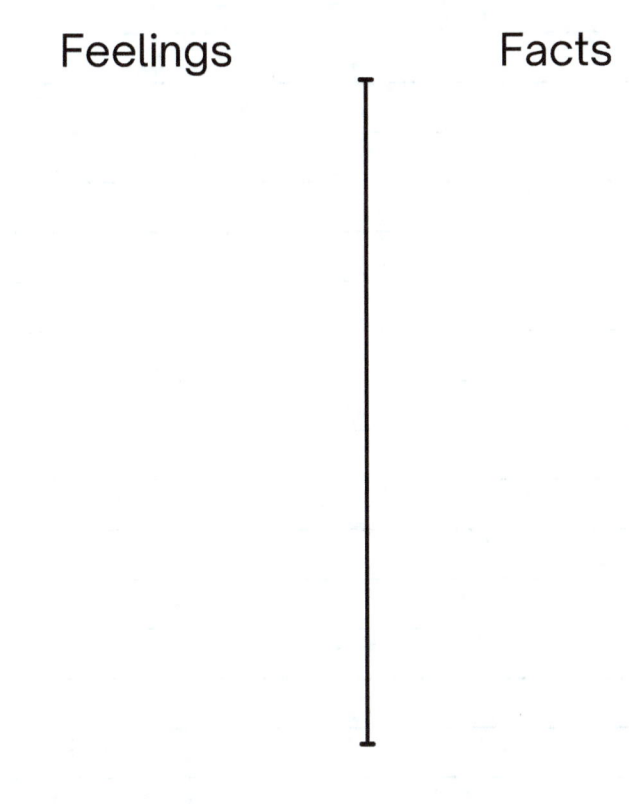

Feelings   Facts

Comforting thought to hold on to:

Situation that triggered the emotions:

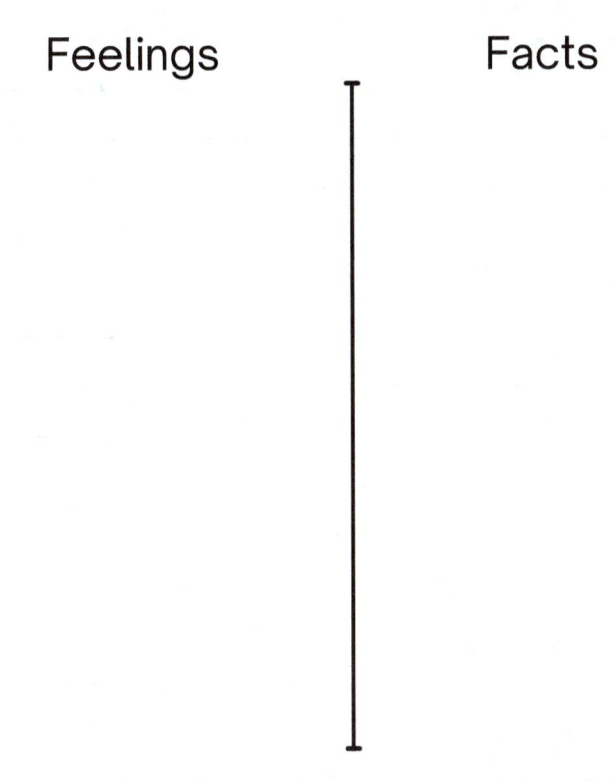

Feelings   Facts

Comforting thought to hold on to:

Situation that triggered the emotions:

Feelings   Facts

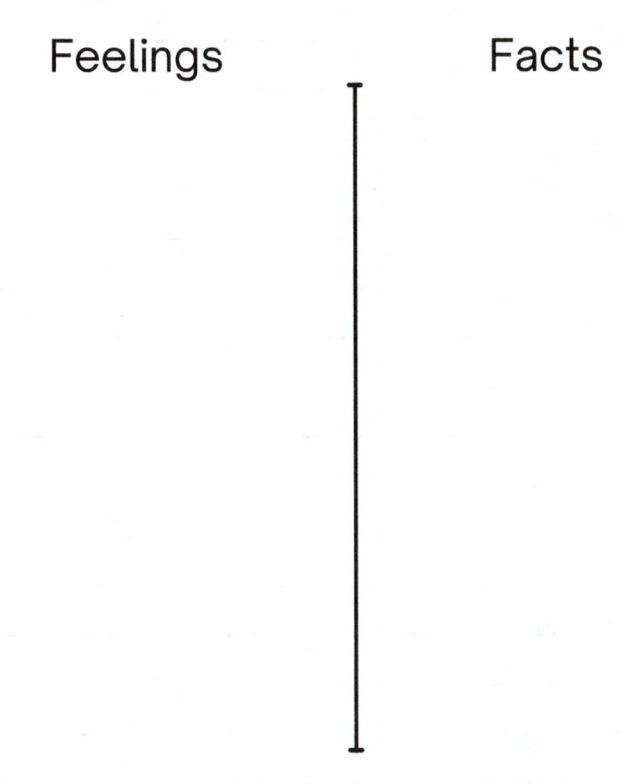

Comforting thought to hold on to:

tuation that triggered the emotions:

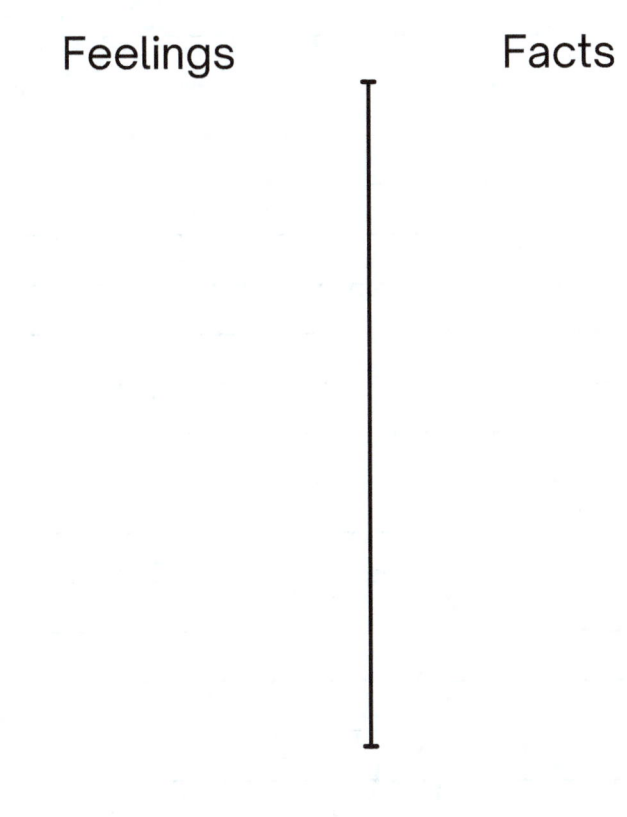

Feelings   Facts

Comforting thought to hold on to:

Situation that triggered the emotions:

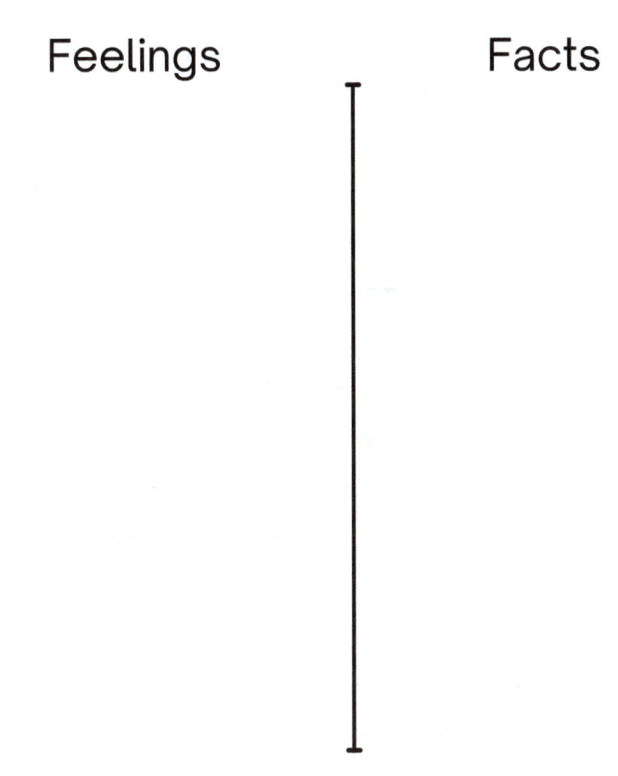

Feelings   Facts

Comforting thought to hold on to:

ituation that triggered the emotions:

Feelings   Facts

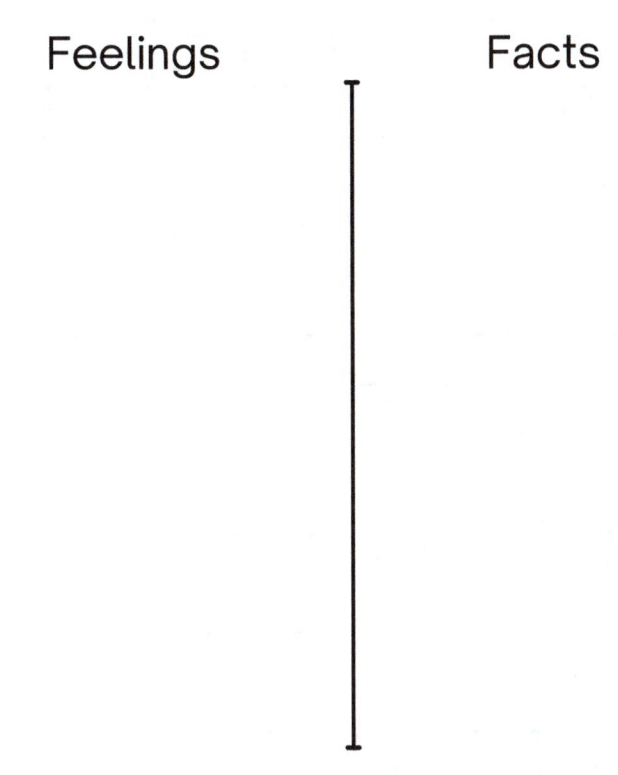

Comforting thought to hold on to:

tuation that triggered the emotions:

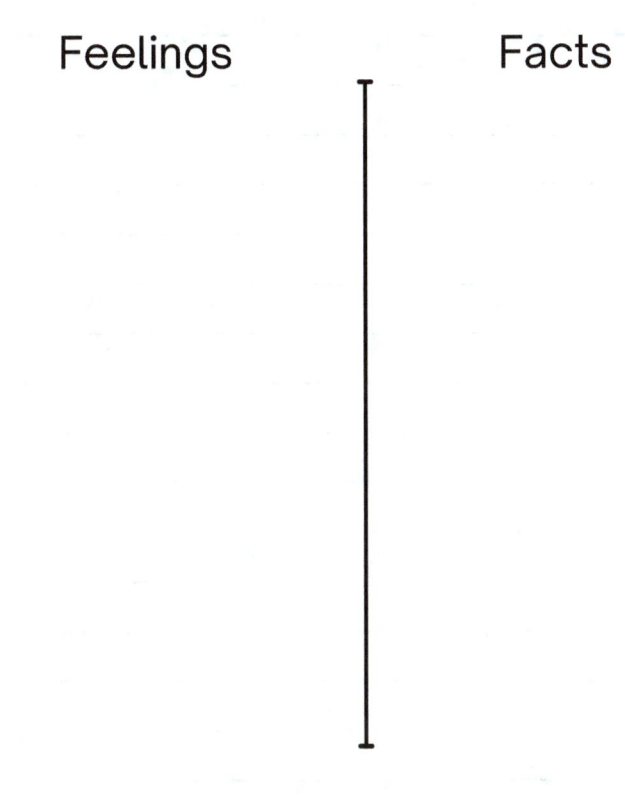

Feelings   Facts

Comforting thought to hold on to:

Situation that triggered the emotions:

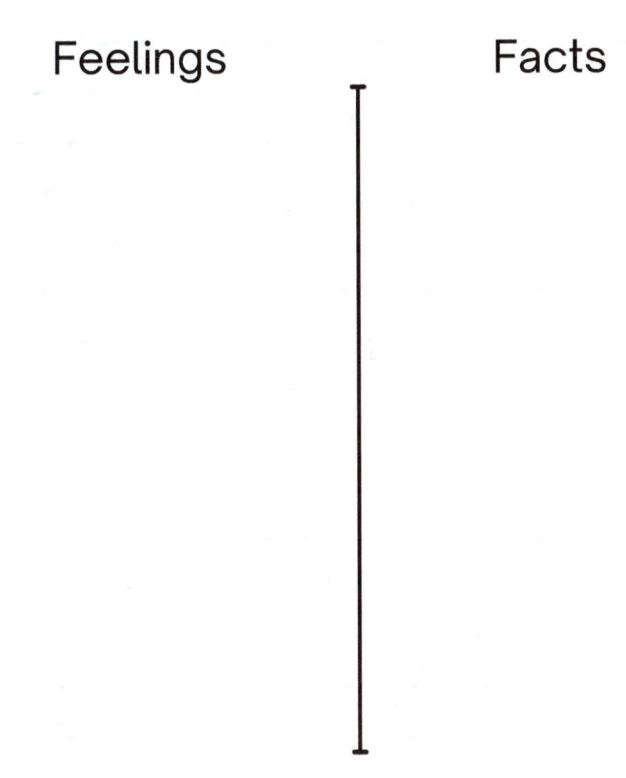

Feelings   Facts

Comforting thought to hold on to:

Situation that triggered the emotions:

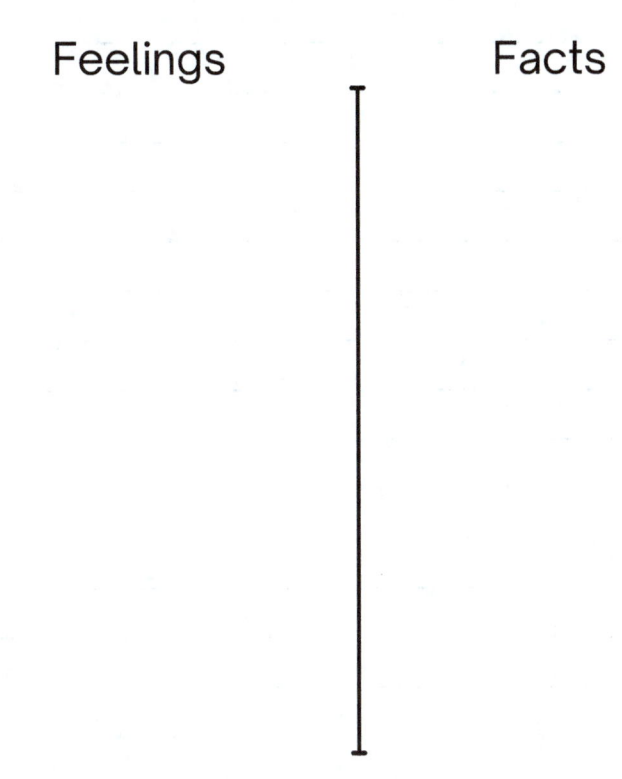

Feelings   Facts

Comforting thought to hold on to:

tuation that triggered the emotions:

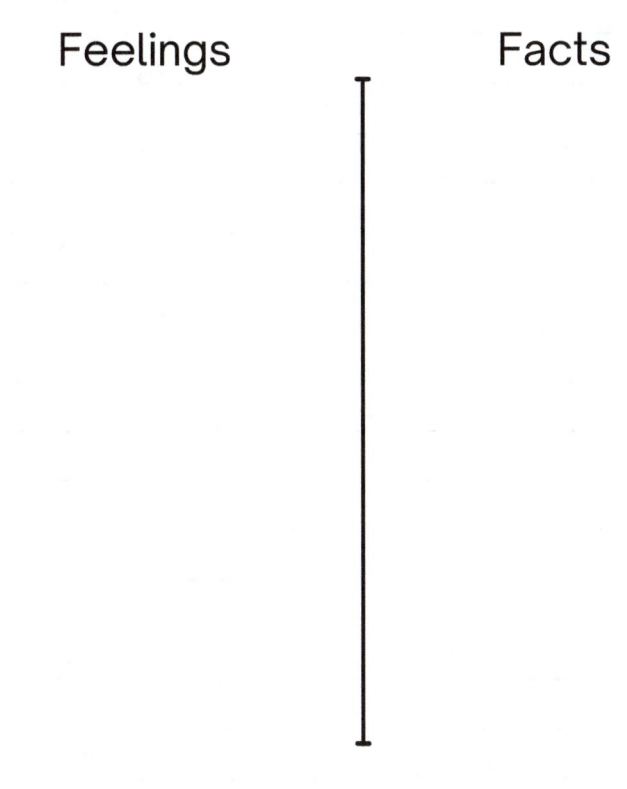

Feelings

Facts

Comforting thought to hold on to:

Situation that triggered the emotions:

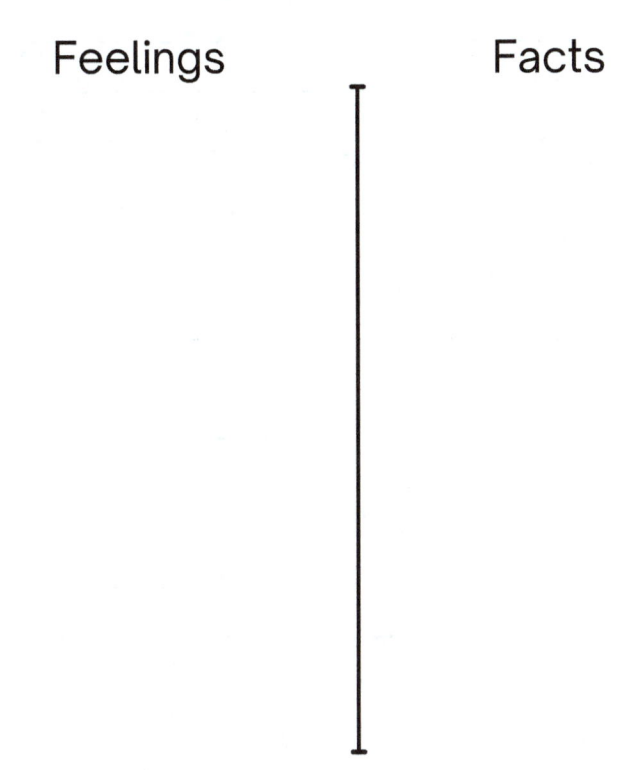

Feelings   Facts

Comforting thought to hold on to:

Situation that triggered the emotions:

Feelings   Facts

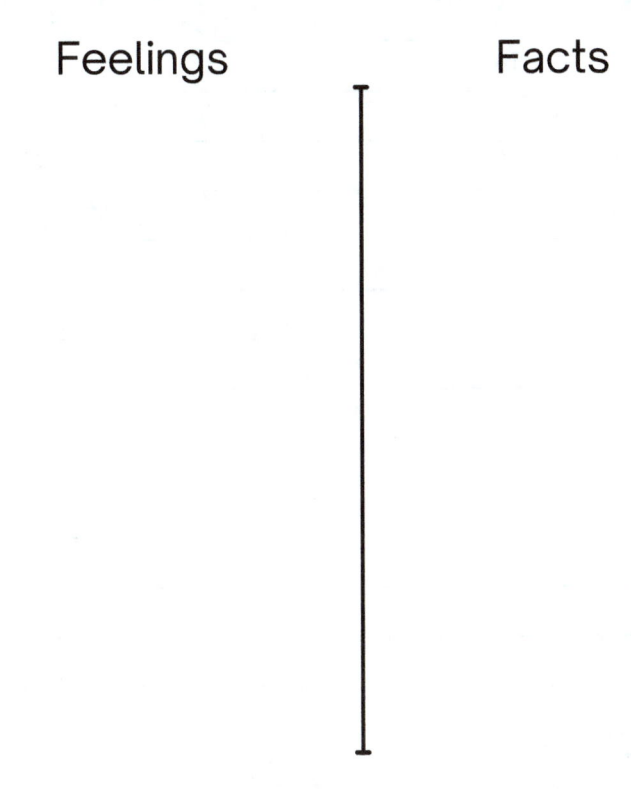

Comforting thought to hold on to:

ituation that triggered the emotions:

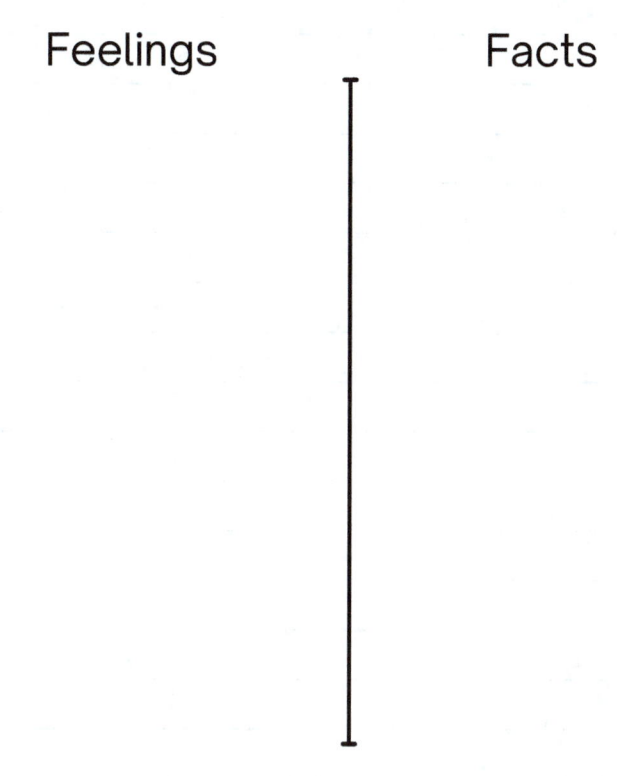

Feelings   Facts

Comforting thought to hold on to:

Situation that triggered the emotions:

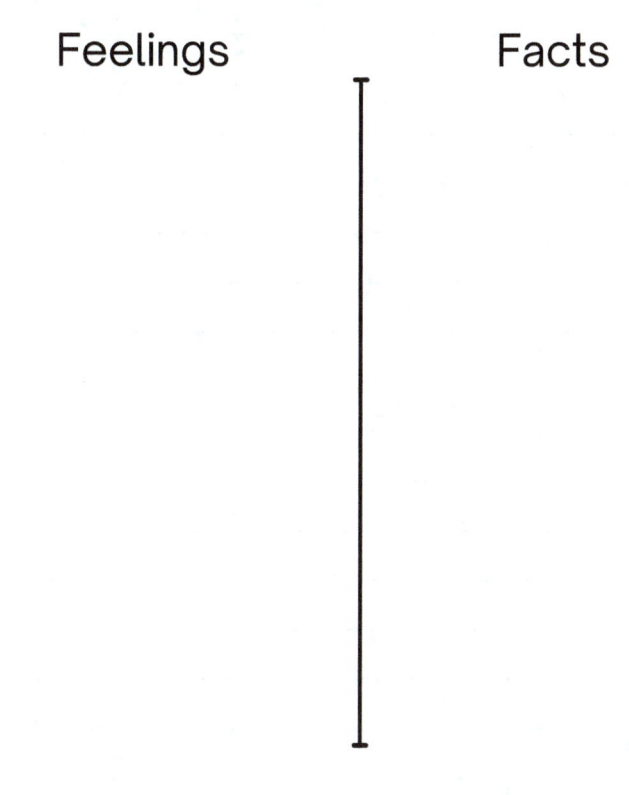

Feelings   Facts

Comforting thought to hold on to:

Situation that triggered the emotions:

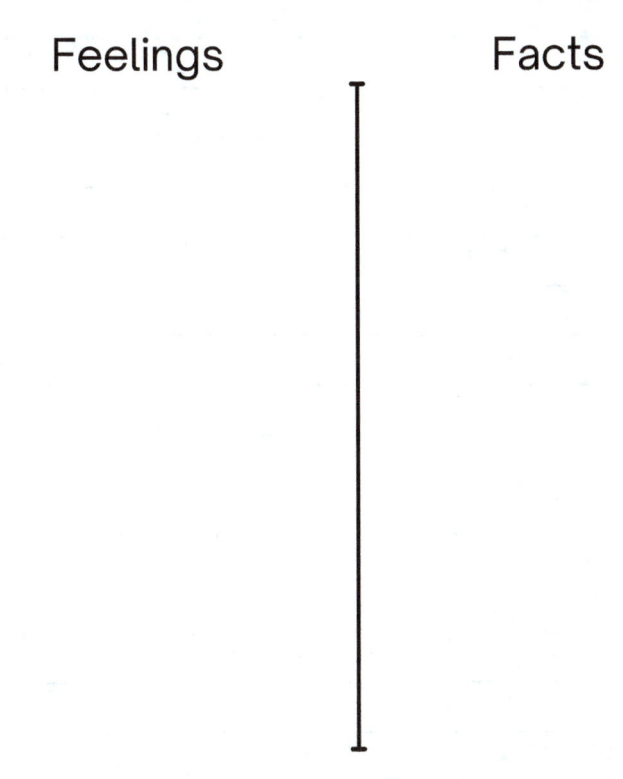

Feelings   Facts

Comforting thought to hold on to:

ituation that triggered the emotions:

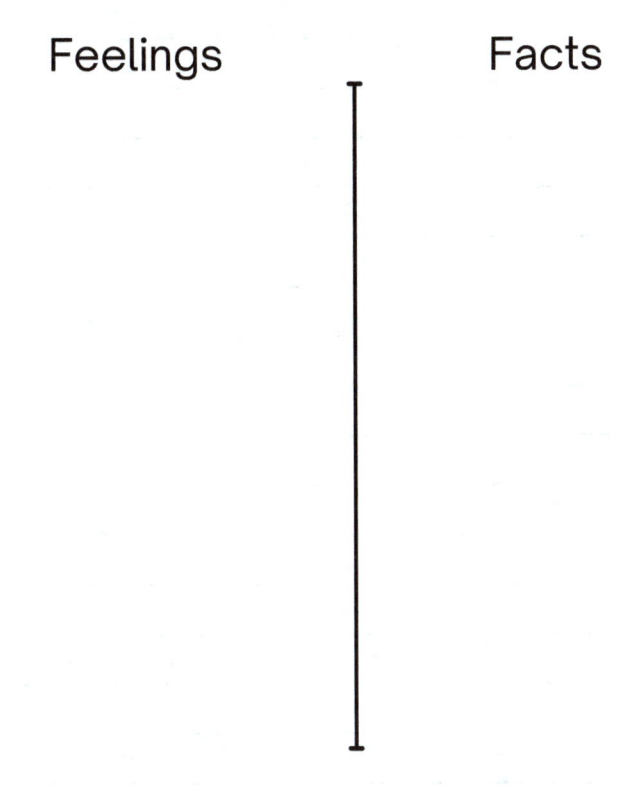

Feelings   Facts

Comforting thought to hold on to:

Situation that triggered the emotions:

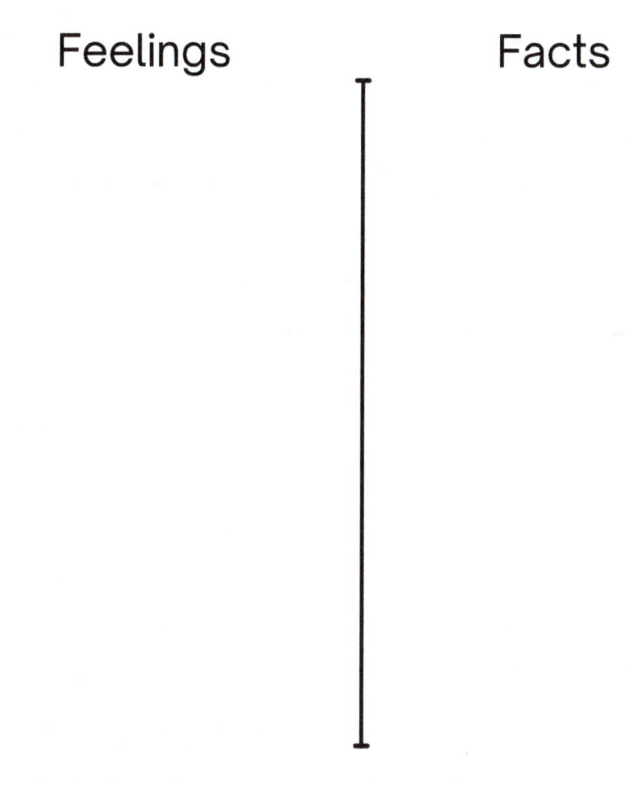

Feelings   Facts

Comforting thought to hold on to:

Situation that triggered the emotions:

Feelings   Facts

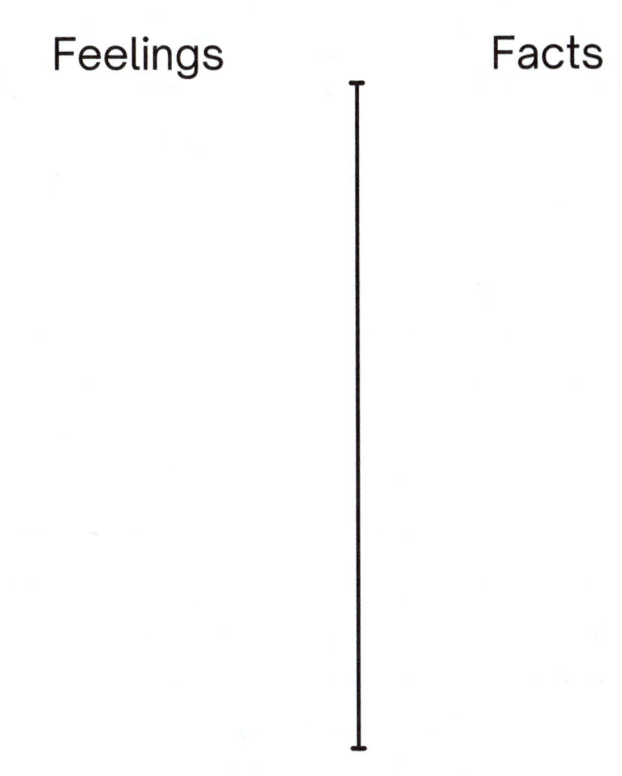

Comforting thought to hold on to:

ituation that triggered the emotions:

Feelings   Facts

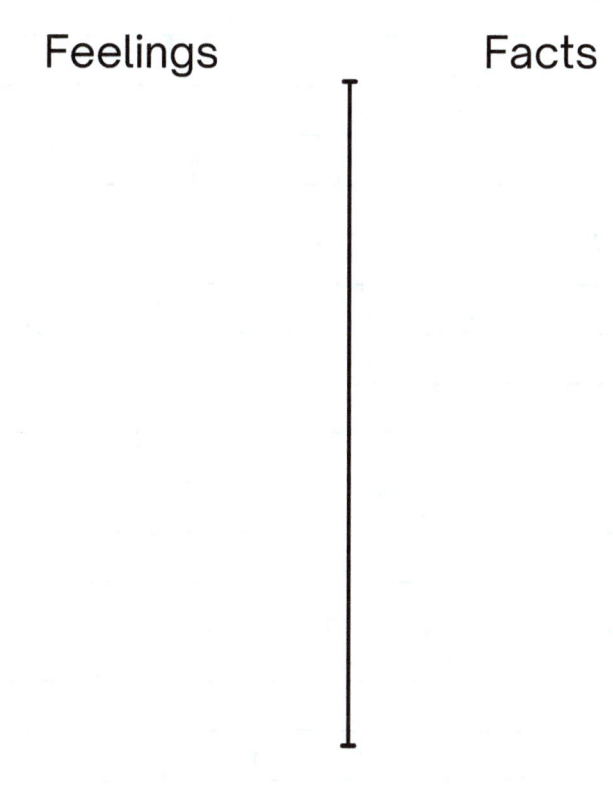

Comforting thought to hold on to:

Situation that triggered the emotions:

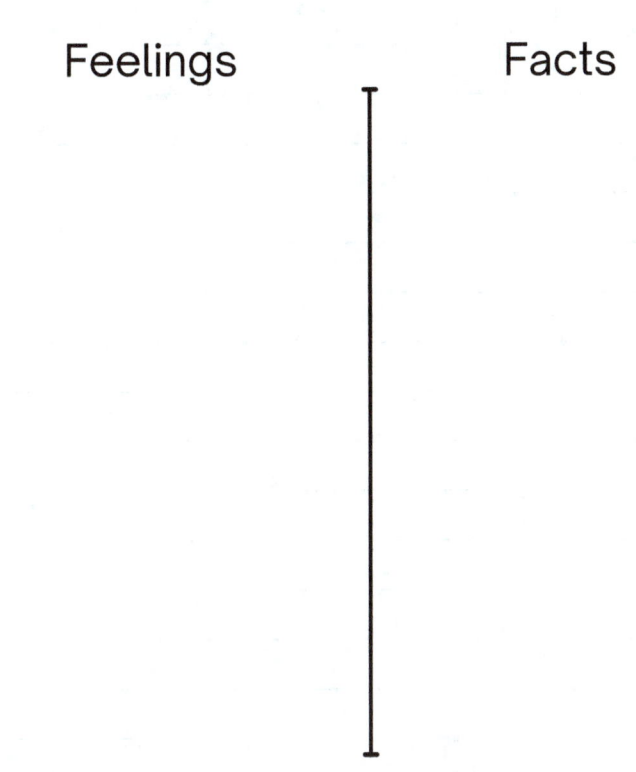

Feelings   Facts

Comforting thought to hold on to:

ituation that triggered the emotions:

Feelings   Facts

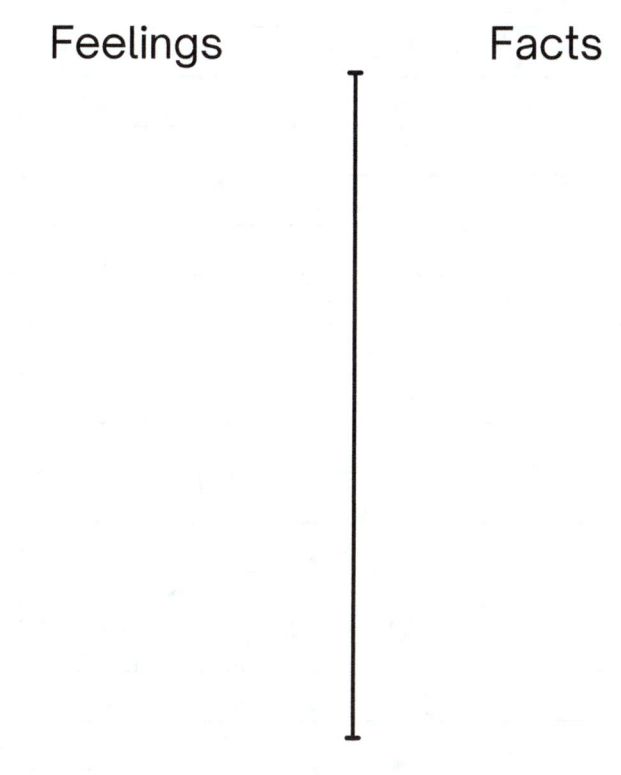

Comforting thought to hold on to:

ituation that triggered the emotions:

Feelings   Facts

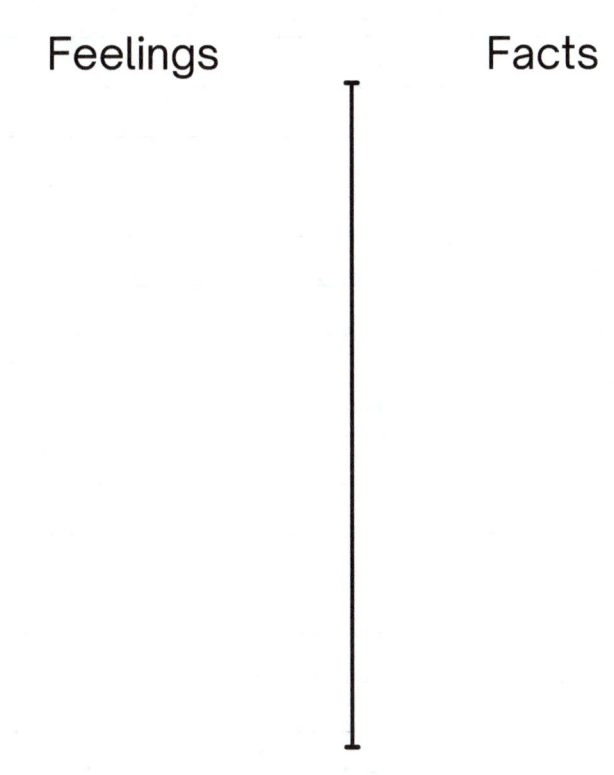

Comforting thought to hold on to:

Situation that triggered the emotions:

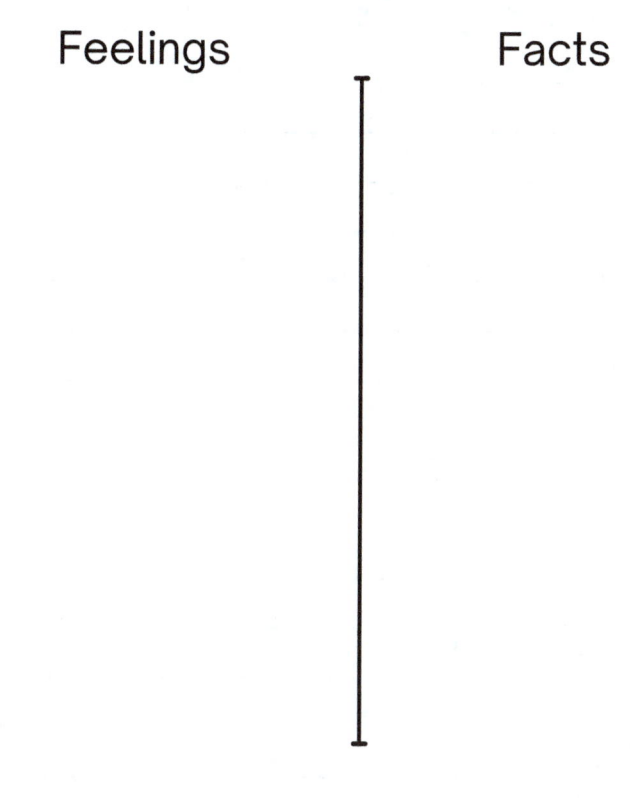

Feelings   Facts

Comforting thought to hold on to:

Situation that triggered the emotions:

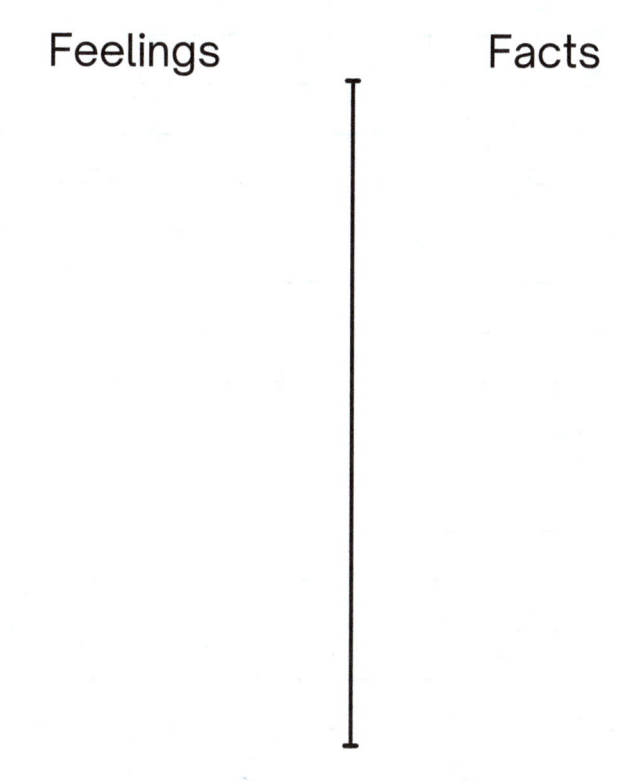

Feelings   Facts

Comforting thought to hold on to:

Situation that triggered the emotions:

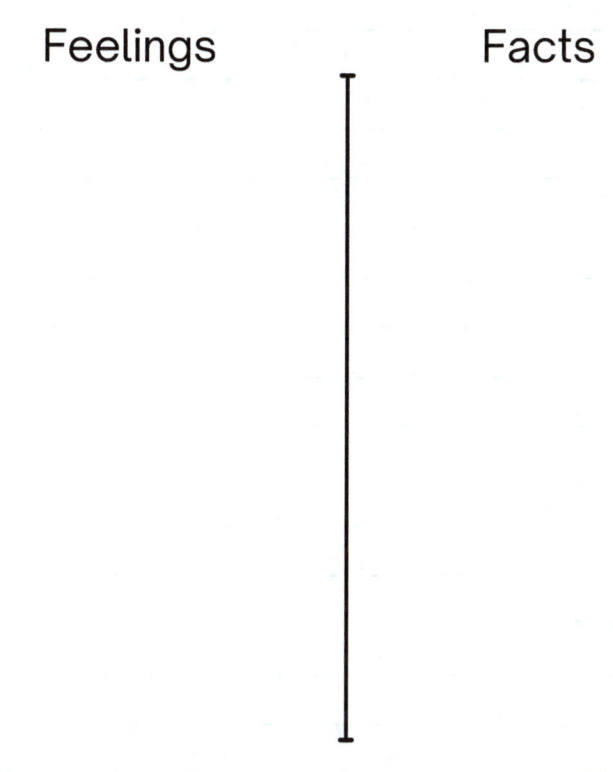

Feelings   Facts

Comforting thought to hold on to:

Situation that triggered the emotions:

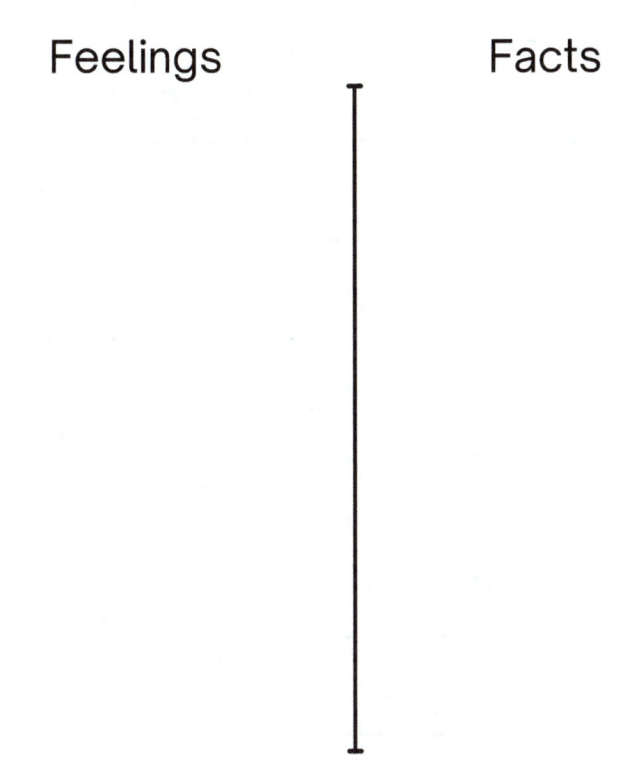

Feelings   Facts

Comforting thought to hold on to:

Situation that triggered the emotions:

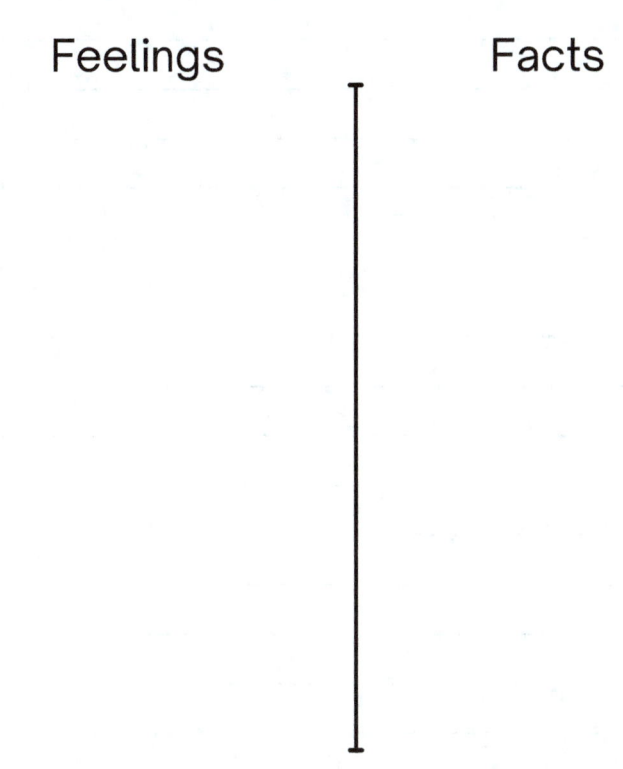

Feelings   Facts

Comforting thought to hold on to:

ituation that triggered the emotions:

Feelings   Facts

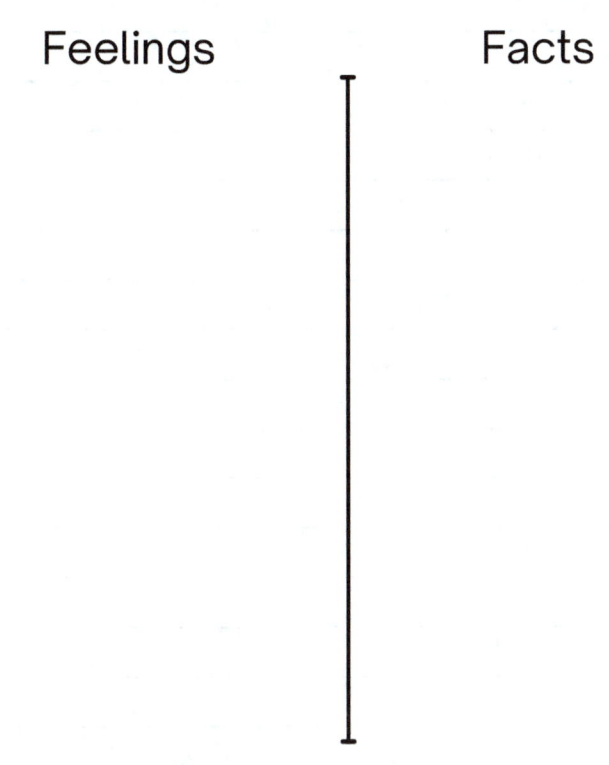

Comforting thought to hold on to:

Situation that triggered the emotions:

Feelings   Facts

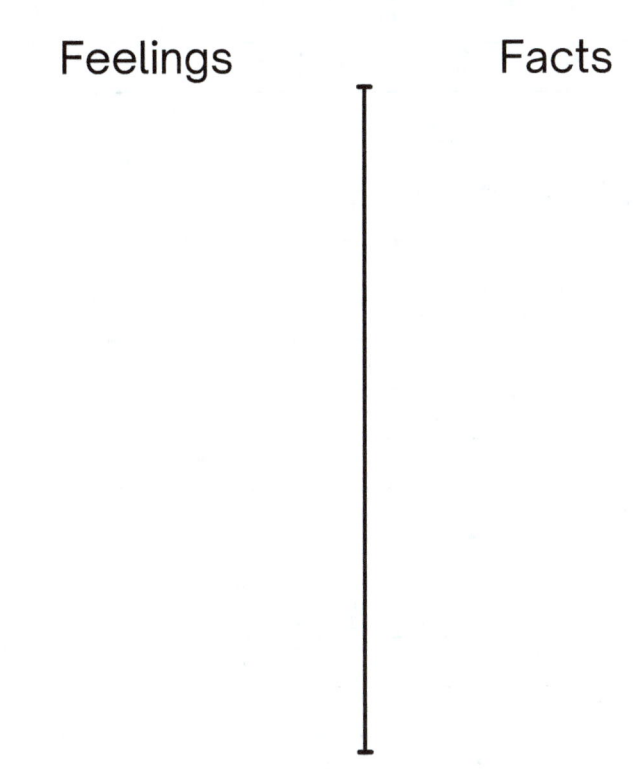

Comforting thought to hold on to:

www.ingramcontent.com/pod-product-compliance
Lightning Source LLC
Chambersburg PA
CBHW070716130626

46553CB00005B/2017

* 9 7 9 8 9 8 8 2 4 0 6 0 0 *